Twenty years ago, while living in California, Richard Adler discovered that he had a genetic form of coronary heart disease due to a hereditary condition, familial hyper-cholesterolaemia (FH), which causes the body to produce more cholesterol than it needs. He has altered his lifestyle through a moderate approach to food, exercise and stress to beat the heart attack that is inevitable unless these risk factors are controlled. So far he has succeeded.

Richard Adler is Honorary Secretary to the Familial Hyper-cholesterolaemia Association, a charity which seeks to alert and inform people like himself who need to change their lifestyle if they are to avoid a heart attack.

He is a designer and writer and lives with his wife and daughter in Oxfordshire.

GW00722622

Beating Your Heart

Richard Adler

CORGI BOOKS

BEATING YOUR HEART

A CORGI BOOK 0 552 12697 7

First publication in Great Britain

PRINTING HISTORY
Corgi edition published 1985

Coronary Heart Disease is quoted by permission of Pitman Publishing Ltd., London.

Prevention of Coronary Heart Disease is quoted by permission of W. B. Saunders and Co., Eastbourne.

Quotations from *The New York Times* are by permission of The New York Times Company (© 1984).

Quotations from the *Archives of Internal Medicine* are by permission of the American Medical Association (© 1984).

COMA report reproduced by permission of The Controller of Her Majesty's Stationery Office.

The publishers thank the following for allowing them to quote from their publications:
Annals of Human Biology, Keith Ball, British Heart Foundation, *British Medical Literature*, *The Daily Telegraph*, *The Economist*, *The Lancet*, *New England Journal of Medicine*, *The Sunday Times* and *The Times*.

This book is set in 10/11pt Times
Corgi Books are published by Transworld Publishers Ltd., Century House, 61–63 Uxbridge Road, Ealing, London W5 5SA, in Australia by Transworld Publishers (Aust.) Pty. Ltd., 26 Harley Crescent, Condell Park, NSW 2200, and in New Zealand by Transworld Publishers (N.Z.) Ltd., Cnr. Moselle and Waipareira Avenues, Henderson, Auckland.

Made and printed in Great Britain by
Hunt Barnard Printing Ltd., Aylesbury, Bucks.

To Elizabeth and Anabelle, with love.

This book is intended as a general introduction to the causes, effects and treatment of coronary heart disease and in no case should any treatment be undertaken without the approval, diagnosis and advice of your doctor.

Acknowledgements

I owe a special vote of thanks to those who personally have helped me to deal with my health. They include Dr R. Yassin, my G.P., whose care and kind advice has been greatly appreciated; Dr J. Mann, Honorary Consultant Physician at the John Radcliffe Hospital in Oxford, who has helped me to lower my blood lipids; and Dr A. Ricards, Cardiologist at the London Heart Hospital, whose knowledge and use of medical technology has been invaluable.

I would like to thank Mary Vun for her advice and assistance in the preparation of the food chart. Also thanks to those doctors who have taken the time to read the manuscript and offer their valuable comments. The goal was to write a book that would be read by laymen such as myself, yet with the medical facts and current opinions reflected as accurately as possible within the text.

'Every affection of the mind that is attended with pain or pleasure, hope or fear, is the cause of an agitation whose influence extends to the heart.'

William Harvey, 'De Motu Cordis', 1628.

1

INTRODUCTION

Look, I know you don't want to hear this . . . but . . . your way of life is probably killing you. You've heard it before and you'll hear it again – endlessly – from your doctor or your family. Even your daily newspaper or favourite magazine will be force-feeding you more facts about cancer, heart disease, diet, exercise, fibre and cholesterol. No institution is safe – the *Financial Times*, the *Wall Street Journal*, *The Times*, and *The Economist* are now saying it. Not to mention radio and TV. There is no escape.

But of course it doesn't apply to you! You're strong as a bull and haven't been sick a day in your life. I know because I didn't want to hear it either. It took just two events to get me to listen . . . but more of my story later.

WHO IS AT RISK?

'Coronary disease is a silent killer. It progresses steadily over decades, gradually narrowing the arteries. Then suddenly, in a matter of seconds, minutes or hours it announces itself, often as death.

'Nearly half of all coronary deaths occur within minutes/ hours of the first onset of symptoms and often outside of hospital. Clearly little can be done at this point in the progress of the disease to affect its outcome'.
Basil M. Rifkind, MD, FRCP, Lipid Metabolism Atherogenesis Branch, Division of Heart and Vascular Disease, US Department of Health

How many of us know someone who has been affected by a heart attack? I should think *all* of us. It's a problem and a fear that never seems to go away – the way polio used to be. Remember polio? Iron lungs and calipers? President Franklin Delano Roosevelt. He had polio. Jonas Salk and others helped to remove that threat from our lives. In New York when summer came you would feel the fear – parents wouldn't talk about it, but it was there for years. But we beat it – we conquered polio.

Heart disease is the greatest killer in the history of the Western world – claiming more lives than polio ever did, more than road accidents, more than cancer. It goes on claiming victims at the rate of 470 a day in Great Britain. *Four Hundred and Seventy a day!* We can't blame a germ or a virus. We don't even have to search for the causes, the way we do with other killer diseases. We *know* the causes. Each one of us can help to prevent it, to control it – and possibly – to cure it. How many of us fear that we might be a victim of a heart attack? You? The fellow opposite you on the train? Me? I know that any person with whom I bring up the subject is instantly full of questions . . . What does it feel like? How do you know? What age? Am I vulnerable?

Indigestion in a man over 40 years scares the hell out of him. Why? Because most of us know too few of the facts about it and most of us are doing nothing to stop it happening to *us*.

'Today Britain has the highest recorded mortality rates for coronary heart disease in the world'.
The Lancet, August 6. 1983

'The fall in mortality from heart disease in the United States, Australia, Belgium, Finland, Canada and the Netherlands began some years ago and is now substantial. Our present rate of mortality from heart disease may be seen as the side-effect of inactivity.'
British Medical Journal, July, 1980.

The amount of research in the past fifteen years has been vast. As a result some people are winning the battle against early death or disability from CHD (coronary heart disease). Deaths from heart disease have fallen over 25 per cent in countries that have informed their people about its causes and cures. Why not Great Britain?

My fifteen-year-old daughter told me that the sermon delivered at her Sunday chapel service was on 'death'. It had been chosen because of the sudden deaths of two fathers that month, both in their early forties and both from heart attacks. The girls in the chapel shared the grief and the fear – most have fathers in their forties and fifties. They were being forced too soon to live with death. What if something could have been done to prevent such deaths? What if these men could have lived to see their daughters grow up, and could have contributed 30 years more to their society? You understand now why you must know the facts and what *you* can do about it, so that you don't become part of that fateful statistic – *470 per day. Every day*. And really, it's not so hard, there are no great sacrifices – just a few small ones. It's worth it.

The international medical profession agrees that CHD is a major killer that can and must be controlled – and *now*. I knew that I was at risk, I analysed my situation and I chose to take action to minimise this risk – to try to do all I could to live a longer, fuller and healthier life.

MY STORY

I was 30 years old. I was on the threshold of an exciting and demanding career in the entertainment business. I had a beautiful house with a swimming pool in Los Angeles, a new car, the warm California sunshine . . . Life was great. But I also had the normal problems of the people around me. I was overweight. I was intense and worked constantly under pressure. I was short-tempered and strong-willed. I ate whatever I wanted of all the available American junk food goodies – hot dogs, hamburgers, ice-cream, pancakes with maple syrup and a side order of bacon or sausage. And then there were the rich business dinners in all the scattered cities I visited in the course of my work.

The first event took place on a warm California evening at a party in Beverly Hills. My host introduced me to a close friend of the family – an eminent cardiologist. We shook hands and as he looked at me the doctor said, 'Please come and see me in my office, I'd like to speak with you'. This took me by surprise as it was the first time I had been chatted up by an eminent cardiologist.

It sounds like a TV hospital soap opera, yet it was my introduction to coronary heart disease (CHD). Now eighteen years later, I am thankful to that doctor for recognising one of the few visual symptoms of CHD – a corneal arcus, the small white ring of accumulated cholesterol around the pupils of the eyes, which occurs in young people who have inherited a type of CHD called Familial Hypercholesterolaemia (FH – see page 42). This meeting changed and saved my life.

The second event took place later that year as I was walking to my car in the parking lot of the Greek Theatre in Los Angeles. I felt a knife-like pain in my side. I could hardly breathe. each breath was agony. In the emergency room at the nearest hospital I was told that I had pleurisy. The pain gradually went away but I had feared the worst – that I was having a heart attack. It was a fear that I didn't want to feel again. I knew some young people who had recently died of heart attacks and strokes. I was scared!

DOCTOR'S OFFICE (TWO MONTHS EARLIER)

When I finally went to see the doctor he took some blood tests and examined me. He then told me in a very gentle. but firm, way that I had to alter my lifestyle or else I was headed for an early death. I was shocked and afraid. I was just beginning to live, I felt infallible, immortal – I had everything in front of me. I was aware that strokes and heart attacks happened – my mother had her first stroke when she was 42 years old – but not to me! In our early thirties, few of us think of our own deaths – and at the tender ages of ten or fifteen (when the first stages of CHD have already begun) hardly anyone contemplates mortality. Most of us feel invincible and immortal – and that's the way it should be. We need to face growing up and the world we live in with strength and energy and optimism.

I went home and my wife confirmed all the changes that she had seen take place in me over the last few years. To illustrate her point she asked me to take off my shirt and have a good look in the mirror. This is what I saw:

RICHARD ADLER – Age: 31. Height: 6 ft. Weight: 190 lb. Appearance: Overweight with visible body fat and a round plump face where there used to be bones and features. Tight. ill-fitting jeans with a stomach hanging over the top. A man who looked in his forties.

This is probably the simplest. most accurate test that you can take: look in the mirror and if you don't *look* fit – you are probably *not* fit.

This statement isn't a major medical breakthrough but if the person *you* see in the mirror looks fit, has decent muscle tone and your honest comment on the reflected image would be, 'he looks good – for his age he isn't in bad shape', then you're an exception to the general rule in Great Britain.

FACT
There has been a progressive increase in the average weight for height of adults in Great Britain over the last 40 years and by 1981 over 40 per cent of middle-aged men and women were overweight. From Rosenbaum, S., Skinner, R. K., Knight, I. B., Garron, J. S. 'A Survey of Heights and Weights of Adults in Great Britain. 1980.'

Annals of Human Biology

What I saw surprised me. I wasn't as slim as I had been three years before when I left Brazil for Los Angeles. I pondered on the strangeness of life. When we lived in Rio I wasn't rich, but active and happy. I walked everywhere. I ate rice and beans, fresh vegetables and fruit. I drank tropical fruit juices – and I ate fish and chicken rather than red meats. I didn't smoke. I didn't drink much. I was relaxed and swam and played sports because I had the time. Now, in 1967, I looked fat, ate too much, and I had aged considerably in my supposedly better environment. I had let Western affluence run away with me.

Being told that I had coronary heart disease and the fact that I could see the physical changes that were taking place made me realise that *I* would have to do something about it. As it seemed that I was suffering from a disease I could neither spell nor pronounce (Familial Hypercholesterol-aemia) and about which I knew nothing, except that you can die from it, I decided to find out some facts – and they shocked me.

FACT:
Every year heart disease kills more people than any other major killer disease. (That includes cancer, infectious diseases and road accidents.)

Fifty per cent of heart attack victims die as a result of the first attack.

Millions of people in the UK have coronary heart disease and are unaware of it, as there are no symptoms until it is advanced.

It is a disease that gives us a false sense of security: 'If it doesn't hurt, I don't have it'. Unfortunately, that's not the case. I had no pain, no obvious signs or symptoms, yet I was close to my first heart attack and – as half of first heart attack victims die – I wasn't happy about my odds.

I hadn't realised that lifestyle was one of the major causes of heart disease. I had assumed that things 'beyond my control' caused heart attacks and strokes. I was wrong. Heart disease can be controlled. It can also be prevented – and possibly, reversed. And all this is within our own control. CHD isn't caused by a 'super-virus' or a bug from a mysterious source. It is a disease of epidemic proportions and it is a direct result of our affluent Western lifestyle. Its causes are: too much food and too rich a diet resulting in overweight; high blood pressure; lack of exercise; smoking; high blood cholesterol levels and stress . . . These are lifestyle causes – man-made reasons for the disease. Most of us are potential victims. At this moment millions of people in the United States and Great Britain have CHD – and most of them don't even know it. Yet this is a disease you don't just catch. You might inherit something that makes you a greater risk – but the fact is that we all help to breed it within ourselves – and the food we eat is one of its principal causes.

That white ring around the pupil of my eye noticed by

the doctor showed that I might have an early, advanced form of atherosclerosis, sometimes referred to as hardening of the arteries.

Atherosclerosis is a narrowing of the coronary arteries by a fatty deposit containing cholesterol which can cause blockages that lead to heart attacks and strokes.

'The problem in dealing with it is it goes on *in* everyone for a long period of time without any signs or symptoms. Then suddenly, in a matter of minutes, because of further blockage one may have angina, chest pain, heart attack or sudden death. It is a terrible frustration that in about a quarter of heart attack victims the first clinical sign of atherosclerosis is also the last and terminates in sudden death.'

Dr R. I. Levy, National Heart and Lung Institute, Bethesda, USA.

There are times in our lives when we tend to sum things up and take a look at ourselves. Usually 40 is the major turning-point, where we realise that we are not immortal and if we are to accomplish what we set out to do, we'd better get on with it – start to put our lives in order – assess what we are capable of accomplishing and what we really want from life. We owe it to ourselves and to our families. For some of us it's too late to begin again, but many are able to steer their lives into new, creative directions, spurred on by the realisation that time is passing.

Serious illness at a comparatively young age snaps you out of youth and forces you to think of the possibility that you might die. The most basic fact that you took for granted – life – suddenly becomes vulnerable, and something you have to work at if you intend to live the normal allotted span.

The first decision that I made was to do something to

control the coronary heart disease from progressing rapidly.

The primary action I was advised to take was to change my eating habits. I had to learn what was good for me and what was bad – and then to substitute good for bad as well as decrease the quantity of food that I was eating. I had to learn the true meaning of the word *moderation*. I never acknowledged it existed – you don't when you're 30. I found it impossible to stop eating the ice-cream. the hot dogs and goodies all at once. I realised that I ate for reasons other than nourishing my body. Eating was a great pleasure and it made me feel good to do it. and three hot dogs made me feel better than one or two. And two cold beers tasted better than one. I was addicted to eating – I had to do it – for the comfort it gave me.

But fear is a tremendous spur and gradually I decreased the amount I ate and began to substitute less fatty (and therefore containing less cholesterol) foods. This was difficult at first. but within a year my eating pattern changed. I developed a *Moderate Diet* (see page 124). Ounce by ounce. I lost weight and didn't put it back on because I had changed my way of eating. I was eating less and substituting good for bad. I had been told that crash diets never work. that once you come off the diet. you'll regain weight immediately. that overeating is a mental problem as well as a physical one.

On analysis. I had been eating foods with high fat, high sugar and high salt content – all of which were bad for me. I started my new lifestyle diet by substituting low saturated fat. high polyunsaturated margarine for butter and skimmed milk for the creamy kind. Both were easy to get used to – and in fact pleasant. I replaced some of the red meat in my diet with chicken and fish – again no major hardship; I reduced my ice-cream consumption – that was difficult; I cut down on chocolate and biscuits and cakes and pastries – with much grumbling. ate more salads and fruit. which I

17

liked; I had fewer fried foods and used corn oils exclusively for cooking and salad dressing.

To my surprise I began to develop a taste for foods that were healthier for my system. I'll tell you how I discovered that – I'd sneakily eaten one of the forbidden foods and suddenly it didn't taste as good as I remembered . . . It's all a question of what you are used to eating. Bad foods might only be a habit. For instance – I can't drink tea with sugar any more; and now I enjoy the taste of the tea or the coffee – more than just the sweetness.

I progressed to cereals with bran and wheatgerm in the morning rather than toast or croissants; substituted fruit and vegetable juices for soft drinks; and low-diet drinks when I wanted a cold drink. I drank decaffeinated coffee (caffeine makes me jumpy) and used artificial sweeteners instead of sugar. I stopped adding salt to my food and used a minimum (if any at all) in cooking. I started to read the labels on tins and packaged frozen foods before I bought them – and I was horrified by what I read – and as a result began eating as many fresh foods as I could. Food labels deceived me by not stating their contents, so I had trouble locating the amounts of saturated fats and types of oils contained in most packaged foods.

The satisfaction of seeing my weight start to fall and my blood cholesterol level fall as well, gave me the incentive to continue my plan not to *diet*, but to develop new eating habits. I ate one biscuit rather than two, a small fries at MacDonalds rather than my normal large one (and usually some of my daughter's portion as well). Second helpings were forbidden and I tried (though I didn't always succeed) not to eat between meals. The taco and hot dog stands became 'off-limits' to me.

OK. We all *think* about doing it – but give me credit, *I did it*. And it really worked.

Exercise was the second necessary factor in my then sedentary life. I bought an exercise bicycle so that I could force myself to get the blood pumping through my system for 30 minutes at a time. It was a big help, but I can't tell you how boring it was – and still is. The only answer is to read the paper while you pedal, or even watch a video. It's not a good time for just your own thoughts and contemplation of life!

This new pattern of living continued for a couple of years but then came a major change. With my family, I left California for Europe where we settled in southern Spain, and with the change of country came a change of diet.

The contrast between the glossy abundance of the supermarkets in Los Angeles and the bustling, colourful street markets of Fuengirola and Marbella came as quite a surprise – happily it turned out to be a good one. There was a bounty of fish fresh from the sea, free-range chickens and the local produce; vegetables and fruits for which the area is famous. And missing from the shops was an enormous variety of red meats and the creamy dairy products we were used to seeing. Instead there were yoghurts, juices and milk so thin and fatless it looked blue. The wine was terrific too, in moderation of course.

So I had left California where the normal diet was bad, for Spain, where the normal diet was healthy, delicious and satisfying. Eventually I left there for England where the normal British diet is diabolical.

'Today Britain has the highest recorded mortality rates for coronary heart disease in the world. All physicians and particularly those concerned with our high coronary mortality rates should press the DHSS to take a much firmer stand in what is considered by nearly every medical authority to be *the fundamental cause of heart disease – our National Diet*.

Keith Ball, Dept of Community Medicine
Middlesex Hospital Medical School,
Central Middlesex Hospital.
The Lancet, August 6, 1983.

'A major campaign to encourage a healthier diet is long overdue in the UK, not only for the prevention of CHD but also because of the growing evidence that our high-fat diet may also be a factor in the causation of cancers of breast and colon.

Ibid., *The Lancet*, February, 1982.

Chips with everything, tempting fat-laden sausages, golden rich butter, full cream milk, glorious double cream, and the justly famous and lethal 'full English breakfast', pasties and puddings, cream teas and Sunday lunch; I love and fear them all – and so should you!

Needless to say, the normal British diet and its temptations undermined my wonderful new willpower. Added to which I found it difficult at that time to obtain skimmed milk and low saturated fat margarine. Fresh vegetables and fruits were more seasonal and more limited than in the sunny climates of California and southern Spain. After six years in Britain I found I had gained a stone and that my blood cholesterol was raised.

One day, pedalling away on my exercise bicycle, I had a pain in my chest. Fear again took me to my doctor.

When I saw Dr Yassin he reminded me that in 1974, when I first became his patient, he had noticed the cholesterol arcus (the white ring round the pupil of my eyes) and my family history and had therefore had my blood lipids tested. At the time my cholesterol was raised and I had been put on a diet which had reduced the level to normal. Due to the British lifestyle and the pressure of new business commitments I had lapsed into my old ways with food and my blood cholesterol had risen again.

Dr Yassin felt that my chest pains were not due to angina. He therefore referred me to a Dr A. Rickards for a *coronary angiogram*.

There are effective and accurate tests to detect high

blood pressure, high cholesterol and other risk factors. Unfortunately there is no perfect way to photograph the *inside* of your arteries from *outside* your body – X-rays just won't do the job. Having an angiogram taken involves having a catheter (a small, tube-like needle) inserted into a vein in the arm or the groin. The catheter is then pushed up through the arterial system past the shoulder and into the heart. A radio-opaque substance is injected through the catheter to the heart and very sophisticated machinery then films the inside of your coronary arteries. This process will tell the true picture, but it is invasive and therefore has its risks. It is never done unless the situation is considered vital by a cardiologist. The whole process involves a half-day, or at the most, overnight, in hospital.

So there I was, lying down in the operating theatre while Dr Rickards and his assistants watched what they had just filmed – my blood coursing, or *not*, through my arteries.

The angiogram confirmed that the narrowing of the arteries was advanced, and it was felt that it had been controlled for the past ten years, or more – and probably hadn't progressed much since I went on my change of lifestyle programme. The cardiologist saw that a secondary artery had been completely blocked by a fatty deposit at approximately that time and that my circulatory system had successfully bypassed that blocked artery. I recalled with a sudden clarity the night at the Greek Theatre in Hollywood when I had been clutched by the terrible pain that had sent me panic-stricken to the Cedars of Lebanon Hospital. The diagnosis by the young intern had been pleurisy. I wonder? . . .

However, as this was an arterial branch rather than a major artery, I had been spared the worst. A few millimetres either way and it might have been fatal. I had been given a second chance. Unfortunately not everyone is that lucky.

As usual, I was full of questions. The cardiologist

explained that the pain in my chest was not caused by coronary heart disease. It could have been caused by one of many things – indigestion, muscular cramp, anxiety. So you see, pain in the chest is not always angina or heart-related pain, but still should prompt you to consult your doctor.

The next step was to put me on a programme of *beta-blockers*. A beta-blocker is an interesting drug. Technically, what it does is to obstruct the beta-receptors – the molecules on the heart muscle which receive the hormonal message to increase heart rate. Because the blockers prevent that stimulation, they decrease heart rate, ease the workload on the heart muscle and consequently lessen pain. They lessen frequency and severity of pain brought on by emotional stress, they lower blood pressure and reduce the oxygen requirement of the heart muscle.

What this actually means is that a beta-blocker reduces the risk of ventricular fibrillation (rapid heart beat) thus helping to avoid a heart attack. It slows down the pulse rate and therefore takes the strain off the heart. It can also act as a mild tranquillizer and, in my case, much of the stress I felt has been lessened by a small daily dose, fortunately without the 'downer' effect of the more commonly pre-scribed tranquillizers.

The cardiologist suggested I continue with my moderate lifestyle, keep my weight at a reasonable level and that I discuss further with Dr Yassin any medical means of lowering my cholesterol.

Dr Yassin next referred me to Dr Jim Mann at the Radcliffe Hospital in Oxford, an Honorary Consultant in Clinical Medicine and head of the Blood Lipid Clinic. This clinic advises people with blood disorders, such as diabetes and high cholesterol, about diets and medicine in order to normalise their blood condition. Jim Mann was not just interested in my case, he was excited to hear of my angiogram. Of course it gave him a perfect record of my arteries *before* the diet and drug programme he proposed. Thus it would give him conclusive proof of the hoped-for success of my treatment, i.e. control and possibly regression. Research has already proved regression of the build-up of the arteries in animals and humans, but conclusive scientific proof is still needed.

His first action was to give me a stress test to observe my heart's reaction to this kind of physical strain. He already knew the state of my arteries and my medical history – he wanted to see how a stress test would diagnose my condition. I pounded away on the treadmill until my eyes popped – but I survived. I was fit.

To supplement the diet of moderation he gave me a small daily dose of Questran – cholestyramine resin, which would lower the level of cholesterol in my blood by 'spongeing up' the cholesterol in the lower intestine before it was re-absorbed into my body through the liver. It did this efficiently, quickly and in my case without side-effects.

Having become more deeply involved I began to want to know more, and tried to find books that could provide answers to the sort of questions a lay person like myself would ask. Unfortunately, I could find no such books available. Those that were written by doctors and professors read like medical books – or the way a doctor might talk to you in his office. The few that were written by laymen were full of technical language and graphs and seemed to express a seriousness that rang false. Therefore I began to read medical periodicals and to ask more questions of my G.P. Dr Yassin, who was very helpful. I also talked to numerous experts in the field, and read countless papers about the subject. Now that I have the knowledge, as well as the personal experience, I would like to pass it on to you.

I have successfully controlled my former excesses and still have the same philosophy – one of a lifestyle of moderation – a life to be enjoyed rather than one of exclusion. I like some things too much to give them up completely, and besides life without them would not be as much fun. Quality of life is as important a factor as the length of our lives. I am not deprived – I feel and look better. I am fitter and have fewer anxieties and fears. And I'm not going to have a heart attack (not if I can do something about it).

Since I had the angiogram three years ago I have been following my programme of diet combined with medicine which, hopefully, is already reversing some of the damage done to my arteries over the last 40 years. I hope I can get you on a programme of first, awareness, and then, treatment – so that you can begin to prevent, or control, or reverse the problem in your arteries.

This book is my story, my battles with stress, weight and diet in modern lifestyle – its pressures, temptations and excesses. So far I'm winning – and I hope I can force you to take a look in the mirror and, if you see a person at risk, to use the questions and answers and the information provided in this book. By so doing, you may save your own life and possibly also save other members of your family.

IDENTIFYING THE RISKS

Although there are usually no symptoms or pain until the disease is far advanced, risk factors are our early warning signals. Heart disease is caused by multiple, interrelated factors, acting together. Prevention and treatment means reducing all of the risk factors that are under our control. Each of us is different, each with a different lifestyle and different degrees of risk. Once you are aware that something is bad for your health you can choose either to avoid it – or to live with the effects and the consequences.

Risk Factors are:

Family history
Smoking
High blood pressure
High blood cholesterol
Physical inactivity
Obesity
Stress
Ageing
Diet
Gender
Cultural and behavioural factors
Personality Type
Diabetes and other disorders
Alcohol
Soft Water
Caffeine and other substances.

If you have any one of the following risk factors you have approximately two times the risk for CHD; (when compared to a normal person of the same age and gender as yourself).

Smoking
High Blood Pressure
High Blood Cholesterol

If you have all these three, your risk is eight times greater ($2 \times 2 \times 2 = 8$). The good news is that these risk factors can be reduced or eliminated!

A FAMILY HISTORY

Some of us inherit a genetic disorder called FH (familial hypercholesterolaemia) which means that the body either produces too much cholesterol, or doesn't remove enough to keep it from accumulating on the walls of the arteries. If either of your parents have heart disease or died at an early age (under 55) from a heart attack or a stroke, you may be affected. At least one person in 500 has FH.

SMOKING

Smoking twenty cigarettes a day increases your risk of dying from Coronary Heart Disease by three times. Once you stop smoking this increased risk is reduced dramatically. Research has linked smoking with heart disease in many ways – all bad!

HIGH BLOOD PRESSURE

If your blood pressure is high then you risk having a stroke or a heart attack. We know the causes of high blood pressure and it is now possible for it to be lowered by diet, drugs, or a combination of the two.

HIGH BLOOD CHOLESTEROL

Cholesterol accumulates on the walls of the coronary arteries, forming atheroma, a substance that may eventually block the flow of blood through the artery. The body manufactures cholesterol for cells and hormones, but too much from dietary sources such as animal fats and dairy products may cause this build-up inside your arteries.

A lower cholesterol level in the bloodstream reduces the rate of heart attack and coronary heart disease. It is a complex subject but, in simple terms, a too high cholesterol level in the blood can be lowered and controlled through a change in your diet, and in some more difficult cases, with drugs.

PHYSICAL INACTIVITY

A lack of beneficial exercise will put you at risk. The right kind will exercise the heart as well as other muscles. This is known as *cardiovascular exercise*. But too much may be just as bad as not enough.

OBESITY

Being slightly overweight might mean only that last year's jeans or dress feels a bit snug, but the point comes where being overweight doesn't just look bad. It is very bad for your heart. Both blood pressure and the level of cholesterol in your blood increase with body weight.

STRESS

Some of us can cope with stress and others can't. Stress stimulates some to work better and gives others ulcers. It drives people to smoke excessively, to drink too much and to lose their tempers too often. When combined with other risk factors, stress increases the risk of CHD.

AGEING

The cholesterol level gets higher as we get older – as does the blood pressure level. We can't control these natural processes but we can be aware of other risk factors we can control – such as smoking, diet and exercise.

GENDER

Men are more at risk than women – a fact that seems to prove that female hormones protect women against some diseases such as heart attacks and high blood pressure. Sadly, the stress of modern life and possibly the Pill have started to erode this natural advantage. Women are having heart attacks at a younger age than ever before.

DIET

Research is constantly establishing links between our national diet and our health. The normal British diet has been shown to be the most unhealthy in the world – too high in saturated fats, salt and sugar – and too low in fibre. High blood cholesterol and high blood pressure (as well as cancer) have been linked to bad diet. Once you know exactly what to eat, how often and how much, you can begin to modify your diet and to decrease your risk of CHD.

CULTURAL AND SOCIAL BEHAVIOURAL FACTORS

There are differences in risk among populations and individuals which are largely social and behavioural, rather than genetic. The soaring increases in heart disease and hypertension from the beginning of this century both in the United States, and in Europe were due to the changes in lifestyles and behaviour. Similarly the decline in CHD mortality in the United States, more than 30 per cent less than the 1968 level, is due to deliberate reversals in lifestyle and attitudes. This contrasts with the constant high incidence of CHD in the UK where lifestyle patterns (diet, smoking, exercise) have not changed as drastically. For example, eastern Mediterranean countries where low saturated fat intake is the norm have lower total cancer mortality rates than England, Wales, Scotland and the United States. This also applies to CHD.

PERSONALITY TYPE

Intense behavioural patterns have been shown to increase the risk of CHD. A person with Type A, or coronary-prone behaviour pattern, has a lifestyle of activity characterised by competitiveness, intense striving for achievement, easily provoked hostility and impatience. People who are relaxed, unhurried, less easily provoked, are defined as Type B, and are less at risk than Type A. Type A people can change the way they react to situations and learn how to recognise and deal with stress.

DIABETES

Diabetics have an increased risk for cardiovascular disease, and the larger group of people with glucose tolerance may also be at increased risk. An increase in blood cholesterol levels along with elevated triglycerides is often found in diabetics, and careful control of diabetes can significantly lower blood lipids.

ALCOHOL

Heavy alcohol consumption is a leading cause of preventable deaths in industrial countries. It is implicated in over 40 per cent of fatal traffic accidents, cirrhosis, suicides, industrial accidents, crimes and murders. And heavy drinking has been proven to increase the risk of CHD. However, evidence has been accumulating that raises the possibility that alcohol, consumed daily in small to moderate amounts, reduces the risk of coronary heart disease. A little a day *may* keep the doctor away.

SOFT WATER

There is now a theory that soft water is bad for you. It has a higher concentration of sodium and seems to dissolve from copper or lead plumbing larger than desirable amounts of some trace minerals such as cadmium, which, along with salt, is a factor in the development of high blood pressure. An EEC directive implemented in 1985, requires that the hardness of water must not be reduced artificially below a set standard.

CAFFEINE

Found in coffee, tea and soft drinks, caffeine may be a contributory factor in CHD. Excessive intake can result in palpitations, nervousness and lack of sleep.

YOUR HEART – HOW IT ALL WORKS

In this book I wanted to explain CHD in straightforward language and terms. But there comes a time when you need to know how your body works and functions – in medical and technical terms. You can read this section through now, or skip it and refer to it later when you would like to know more about your body, especially your heart, blood and circulatory system.

HEART

The heart is a double-pump about the size of your fist. The main veins of the body send the blood into the right side of the heart and it is then pumped into the lungs. The left side receives the blood returning from the lungs and pumps it out through the arteries to the rest of your body. This blood is oxygen-rich. It is circulated through the left ventricle and when it returns to the right side of the heart it has lost its oxygen and contains waste products such as carbon dioxide.

It is venous blood that reaches the lungs through the right ventricle of the heart where it gives up the carbon dioxide for oxygen. Strong, healthy lungs are needed to fill the blood with the fresh oxygen required by all the cells and tissues of the body.

The heart is made up of the heart muscle and two valves on each side of the heart. Each side is made up of two chambers – the atrium and the ventricle. The atrium receives the blood and allows it to flow into the ventricle during diastole, the period of relaxation. The powerful ventricle pumps the blood into the main blood vessel. The valves stop the blood from flowing back into the ventricle from the vessels.

The heart muscle depends on its supply of oxygen for its operational efficiency. If deprived of oxygen, as in a heart attack, it will stop functioning within one or two minutes.

Heart contractions are fired by a small electric current, generated by a collection of cells in the upper part of the atrium, known as the sino-atrial node. The electric signal produced is reflected in the rate of the heart beat and the pulse. This is controlled by the brain which controls the signals to the sino-atrial node. It can also regulate the amount of blood that returns to the heart and its output of blood.

ARTERIES

The coronary arteries provide the heart with its supply of blood. They are branches of the aorta, the main artery, through which your heart pumps the blood around your body. Each of the two coronary arteries divide into two major branches and then into small arteries and capillaries. Some of the smaller arteries are interconnected, so if the blood supply diminishes through one major artery, the other will take over the flow of blood through these smaller blood vessels.

All blood vessels are lined with a smooth tissue (endo-thelial lining) which prevents thickening or clotting of blood within the vessel. The arterial system is like a tree with large and small branches and normally the passage between the arteries is smooth and wide so that blood can pass through freely. Atherosclerosis is a general medical term for diseases of the arteries which include the process

HAY FEVER
No Need To Suffer
by COLIN JOHNSON & DR ARABELLA MELVILLE

Every Spring and early Summer in Britain alone, eight million normally healthy people suffer from hay fever. At best, their symptoms are irritating and annoying, at worst they are severely life-limiting. The great majority of those people need not suffer at all.

Hay Fever – No Need To Suffer not only brings a welcome message of hope for the victims of hay fever, it also offers sound practical advice – based on the authors' own experience – on how to beat this handicapping disease, which normally affects people in their most active years.

Conventional medicine has attempted some answers to the problem over the years, but they are incomplete, and some of them are actually harmful. More and more, it is being realised that the real answers lie in the alternative, or complementary, approaches now readily available, for example through homeopathy or acupuncture. *Hay Fever – No Need To Suffer* points the way to those answers, and promises lasting relief to the millions of people who suffer from this truly environmental disease.

0 552 12480 X   £2.50

A LIST OF HEALTH BOOKS
AVAILABLE FROM CORGI

WHILE EVERY EFFORT IS MADE TO KEEP PRICES LOW, IT IS SOME-
TIMES NECESSARY TO INCREASE PRICES AT SHORT NOTICE. CORGI
BOOKS RESERVE THE RIGHT TO SHOW NEW RETAIL PRICES ON
COVERS WHICH MAY DIFFER FROM THOSE PREVIOUSLY ADVERTISED
IN THE TEXT OR ELSEWHERE.

THE PRICES SHOWN BELOW WERE CORRECT AT THE TIME OF GOING
TO PRESS (MAY '85).

*All these books are available at your book shop or newsagent, or can be ordered
direct from the publisher. Just tick the titles you want and fill in the form below.*

CORGI BOOKS, Cash Sales Department, P.O. Box 11, Falmouth, Cornwall.

Please send cheque or postal order, no currency.

Please allow cost of book(s) plus the following for postage and packing:

U.K. Customers—Allow 55p for the first book, 22p for the second book and 14p for
each additional book ordered, to a maximum charge of £1.75.

B.F.P.O. and Eire—Allow 55p for the first book, 22p for the second book plus 14p
per copy for the next seven books, thereafter 8p per book.

Overseas Customers—Allow £1.00 for the first book and 25p per copy for each
additional book.

NAME (Block Letters) ....

ADDRESS ....

....

in which this lining of the arteries thickens with a deposit of fatty plaque and cholesterol. The earliest signs of atherosclerotic plaque is a barely visible yellowish streak that begins in childhood. In a long and complex process this fatty streak develops into plaque which may eventually obstruct the flow of blood within the artery. The plaque contains crystals of cholesterol.

The location of plaque is usually in the divisions and curvatures of the arterial system – on the twists and turns rather than on the straightways. As blood flows past this plaque it picks up and develops more bulk. High blood pressure and a high blood cholesterol level helps it to grow larger and thicker. In some people this process may be a normal part of ageing but the risk factors we discussed earlier speed-up the atherosclerosis. As this fat build-up is not normal to the arterial wall it produces an inflammatory reaction in the surrounding tissues. Some blood vessels rupture and form scar tissue when they heal. Tissue may die and calcium deposits form and further stiffen the artery wall adding to the plaque, which as it grows traps more fats and cholesterol from the blood as it flows by. The sections of the arteries affected tend to lose their elasticity and their ability to expand freely as blood is pumped. This fatty deposit in the lining of the arteries is called atheroma.

The 'furring up' of the arteries (atherosclerosis) gradually narrows the artery and restricts the flow of blood. This process may take decades before we ever know about it. The heart may pump a bit harder to force the blood through these arteries and thereby raise the blood pressure, but it is gradual, until the artery is obstructed by more than 50 per cent. When the blockage increases to 70 per cent or more a critical point is reached. The blood flow to the heart is slowed – small tears can develop in the lining of the artery. The tears might bleed which, in turn, may cause clotting.

The clots collect on the wall of the artery or pass through

and may collect elsewhere or block some smaller blood vessel.

Clotting in coronary arteries may lead to a partial blockage of the blood to the heart; the heart muscle does not receive the necessary oxygen in the area supplied by the blood vessel, and without sufficient oxygen a muscle will die. The heart responds with its chemical mechanism (autoregulation) to stimulate blood vessels to furnish more oxygen and to tell the brain it needs more oxygen. When this fails the nerve endings signal that fact in the form of heart pain, or angina. It's that dreaded sharp pain in the chest that for many of us is the first signal of CHD.

If the artery is partially blocked and the body can find a way to pump more oxygen to the heart, the pain is temporary – a spasm or a contraction – but if the coronary artery is blocked, you have a heart attack. The blood flow to the heart and to the brain is interrupted, and in 50 per cent of heart attacks the patient dies.

The medical term for a heart attack is *Myocardial Infarction*, which means the heart muscle supplied by the blocked artery does not get enough oxygen and other nutrients, and begins to die. Any narrowing of the arteries will deprive the heart, brain or other organs of oxygen, and tissue may die. To help the injured heart muscle to heal, smaller blood vessels re-route blood through the damaged area. Some of this collateral circulation might have started long before the heart attack happened, in order to take on some of the blood flow from the coronary blood vessels narrowed by atherosclerosis.

BLOOD

Blood is made up of red and white cells and smaller cells called platelets. They are suspended in plasma which carries chemicals and nutrients around the body. When the blood comes in contact with an injured surface a complex change in the fluidity of the blood occurs – the platelets and other cells adhere together and they clot. This prevents further bleeding.

If the lining of the arteries is damaged by an ulcer or by atherosclerosis, a clot or thrombus may form. Chemicals are produced causing the artery to contract. A clot in the arteries may cause a spasm (a contraction) which will lead to anginal pain or a heart attack (coronary thrombosis) where the artery is completely blocked. If the platelets clump together and form a thrombus, pieces of the clot may break away and lodge further along in smaller branches of the artery and cause pain or blockage. This tendency for the platelets to clump together may be a serious problem.

Fats are made up of fatty acids. They are absorbed through the gut and then travel as triglycerides in the lymph vessels to the venous system. They enter the circulation and are carried to the liver. Part of the liver's function is clearing the triglycerides from the blood.

Cholesterol is present in almost every cell. Bile salts are produced from cholesterol and are very important in digestion. Cholesterol is a base for the production of hormones by the body. If there is too much cholesterol in the body from diet, or if the body itself produces too much cholesterol and bile salts, they may find their way through the fine inner lining of blood vessel walls into small lymph vessels which are a fine network in the walls of arteries. The higher the blood cholesterol level the more cholesterol may be filtered through blood vessel walls. Also, the higher the blood pressure, the more force is exerted to move cholesterol across the arterial wall.

When both the cholesterol level and blood pressure are normal the cholesterol will filter through the arterial wall to the lymph vessels. If cholesterol is high, more cholesterol is filtered through the arterial wall. At some point this increased amount of cholesterol will not be able to pass across the wall and will begin to 'plug up the filter' at certain points. This will accumulate and result in fatty deposits of plaque. Now the surface of the arterial inner wall will be irritated and passing fats and cholesterol might stick to it, causing atheroma, or atherosclerotic plaque. At first this is a fatty streak but it will inflame the surrounding tissue. It is the first step to the eventual blockage of an artery.

Cholesterol is a waxy, organic, chemical substance which like fat, does not dissolve in the blood. The blood lipids, cholesterol, phospholipid and triglyceride, all need protein to allow them to circulate in blood plasma – to make them soluble. Therefore the blood lipids form lipoproteins and it is through these that most fat enters and leaves the plasma. There are three major classes of lipoproteins in blood plasma. They are VLDL – very low density lipoprotein (accounting for the majority of the plasma triglyceride); LDL – low density lipoprotein (accounting for about 70 per cent of plasma cholesterol); and HDL – high density lipoprotein (triglyceride and cholesterol concentration is low, about 20 per cent).

LDL deposits cholesterol on the arterial walls and HDL functions as a scavenger in the blood and helps to remove the cholesterol from the blood and the body.

Hyperlipidemia is an increased plasma concentration of cholesterol or triglycerides, or both. A blood test will determine if the level of the blood fats is high, and whether it is cholesterol or triglyceride. Plaque in arteries is made up of two-thirds cholesterol and one-third triglyceride.

A STROKE

A stroke is directly related to the same blocked condition of the coronary arteries. Angina or a heart attack may occur when the blood and oxygen supply to the heart is interrupted. A stroke occurs when the blood supply to the brain is stopped. This is caused by a blood clot inside a cerebral artery, or possibly by a clot that has formed further up the artery and has broken away from an arterial wall. Cerebral thrombosis is the blocking of one of the brain's arteries. When a wandering blood clot becomes wedged in one of the cerebral arteries it is called a cerebral embolism. When a clot plugs a cerebral artery, doctors call the condition cerebrovascular occlusion.

A stroke can also occur when an artery in the brain bursts. This is called a cerebral haemorrhage. Cells fed by the artery are deprived of blood and cannot function. The blood from the burst artery forms a clot which may interfere with brain tissue and function and cause mild or severe symptoms such as loss of speech, sight and movement.

This is most likely to occur when the patient has a combination of atherosclerosis and high blood pressure. A stroke causes nerve cells in the brain to lose their function and the bodily controls regulated by these cells cannot function either. If the body cannot repair the damage within a few minutes the brain cells die as they need an ample and continuous supply of oxygen-rich blood. Injured brain cells cannot regenerate – therefore the best cure, once again, is prevention of stroke through modification of the risk factors.

Although I'm most concerned with coronary heart disease, there are other heart diseases which are not related to atheroma of the coronary arteries.

Rheumatic heart disease is much rarer now than it used to be. An infection in childhood is followed later in life by a disease where the valves of the heart are scarred and deformed. Antibiotics can be prescribed to treat the initial childhood infection, and long-term treatment will prevent recurrence. Recent developments in open heart surgery can often cure defective valves.

Congenital defects are malformations of the heart or its

major blood vessels by abnormal development of the embryo. Some are hereditary, others may be caused when a pregnant woman is exposed to diseases, such as German measles, or to chemical poisons. These defects may include holes in the walls of the heart or defects in the arteries; progress in cardiovascular surgery has made it possible to correct many of these.

CORONARY SPASMS

Arterial spasms can induce a heart attack. It is probable that the spasms are connected with atherosclerosis and blood clots. What causes a spasm? Popular theory is that when a blood cell is ruptured, platelets collect at the site of the injury and plug the rupture temporarily while the body starts the longer-term natural repair. Platelets secrete thromboxane A_2 which induces the formation of blood clots and causes blood vessel walls to constrict. But abnormal platelets are present in patients who have recently had a heart attack and they secrete large amounts of thromboxane A_2. These and other chemicals may induce a spasm or blood clot. Research into the control of these clot-inducing chemicals is well under way. Aspirin is thought to block the body's production of thromboxane A_2. Sudden death or arteriovasospasm may occur without underlying atherosclerosis – it is most common in young women and the cause of coronary spasm is unknown.

VENTRICULAR FIBRILLATION

A normal, healthy heart beats regularly at between 60-90 beats a minute at rest. During exercise or excitement this may rise to as much as 150 beats a minute. An electrical fault (from nerve cells or brain) in the atrium or ventricular chambers of the heart may cause the heart to beat as rapidly as 350 beats per minute. The contractions of the heart become chaotic and it becomes inefficient as a pump, as there is no time between beats for it to fill. Adequate circulation cannot be maintained and the supply of blood and oxygen to the brain is cut off. The rapid beat can be stopped only by a strong electric shock to the heart (using a cardiac defibrillator). This condition is known as *atrial tachycardia* and *ventricular fibrillation*. Fibrillation is disorganised contractions of the heart muscle when different parts of it take up independent contractions. Irregular heart beat is very common in the acute stage following a heart attack and it can be controlled with drugs such as beta-blockers. Therefore, if a doctor is aware of this problem it can be dealt with. Unfortunately it can happen to people without any sign of heart disease and results in sudden death. The cause is often unknown. Fibrillation can be caused by stress or excitement, too much alcohol, coffee, pills or drugs. It is an unusual type of attack and if no electrical or chemical impulse within our body tells it to stop, death occurs rapidly. Sometimes, although the artery may not be severely narrowed, a passing blood clot or a sudden unexplained contraction of the artery may stop the blood flow to the heart. Emotional stress may cause the heart to become 'electronically unstable'.

A HEART ATTACK

WHAT DOES IT FEEL LIKE?

The warning pain, angina pectoris, felt when the heart isn't getting enough blood with the needed oxygen, is a pain from the heart muscle itself. It is a gripping, burning, choking pain in the chest with pressure and pain behind the breastbone, which often extends up to the left shoulder, to the neck and down the left arm or hand. It is often associated with breathlessness and, quite understandably, acute anxiety. It usually occurs during or following

39

exertion or excitement, emotional stress, or after a big meal. It has been known to occur in the morning when walking in cold weather, and sometimes at night awakening from sleep. It can last from 30 seconds to a few minutes and subsides during rest and calming down. No severe chest pain should be ignored – it is one of the rare warning signals we get. If it happens, call a doctor. Any unexplained chest discomfort, followed by weakness, paleness and fatigue, especially in middle-aged men or post-menopausal women, should prompt a visit to your doctor.

If you're like me, I'm sure within five minutes of reading this you are likely to develop chest pains and will break out into a sweat! Obviously all chest pains are not necessarily a warning of a heart attack. Tension, emotional upsets, excessive physical activity or stress will only precipitate a heart attack if you already have an advanced case of atherosclerosis – that is if your arteries are already blocked.

But any symptom occurring in the upper part of the body that is provoked by exercise and relieved by rest should raise a suspicion of angina. Short-lasting stabbing pains in the heart area may simply be a case of indigestion, especially in males under 30 or females under 40. The pain may also be caused by air trapped in the colon or stomach, caused by nervous eating and swallowing excess air. It's difficult to take a deep breath and it may scare the hell out of you. It usually lasts only a few seconds, less than a minute, is unrelated to physical exertion or excitement and is often felt while sitting. We've all had the sensation of stitches in our sides or pains in our stomachs – serious angina is different.

A nagging, constant pain between the ribs and the breastbone that increases with movement of the arms can be arthritis of joints between the ribs and vertebrae. Neuralgia or a pinched nerve will cause a tensing of the muscles between the ribs with severe pain – it can last for days. Pleurisy will do the same, as will shingles, fibrositis,

40

stomach ulcers, hernia or pneumonia.

The fatty build-up within the walls of the arteries is what we must prevent, control and, if possible, reverse.

WHEN DOES IT BEGIN?

As atheroma cannot be diagnosed by X-ray, only the risk factors can imply some development of narrowing of the coronary arteries. We know it begins when we are very young – the reason we know this is through autopsy. This is a rather grisly subject but it is the only way I can explain how we know that atherosclerosis affects the very young. Doctors involved in research have known for a long time that bad diet can cause atherosclerosis, but scientific knowledge needs clinical verification and this is a long, complex process as certain criteria must be met to establish clinical proof. And as you can't examine a person's arteries without a serious medical reason to do so, the only opportunity of seeing if a person has atherosclerosis has been after they are dead. Therefore during the last 30 years pathologists have been observing the coronary arteries of accident victims, people who die prematurely, and young soldiers killed in action during the Korean and Vietnam wars.

In post-mortems of young accident victims in the United States there was a much larger occurrence of fatty streaks in their coronary arteries than in those of Far Eastern or African natives of the same age. During post-mortem examinations of young American soldiers in the Korean war it was discovered that fatty streaks and early plaques were present in 77 per cent and that 15 per cent had a narrowing of at least one coronary artery to 50 per cent of the original opening. When compared with the arteries of Far Eastern men, it was apparent that something was causing this premature obstruction – as the average age of the victims was under 20 years. It was discovered that difference in diet was the cause.

41

RISK FACTORS – A DETAILED STUDY

A FAMILY HISTORY OF HEART DISEASE AND STROKES

'FH is a very specific inherited genetic condition – if you inherit a single gene for familial hypercholesterolaemia from one parent you will inherit the condition. A conservative estimate is that one in 500 is affected, which makes it quite a common condition, probably at least 100,000 people in this country have it. Many cases go unrecognized and the outlook for them, if untreated, is bad.

On average about 50 per cent of men with this condition will have had a coronary by the age of 50 and about half of those will probably have died. By the age of 60 the figure is 85 per cent. For women the figures are 12 per cent by age 50 and 57.5 per cent by age 60. These figures apply if someone had not had treatment. Obviously we believe and indeed there is a considerable amount of evidence to back up our belief, that these figures are greatly improved with treatment.'

J. I. Mann, Hon. Consultant Physician, John Radcliffe Hospital, Oxford

HOW I INHERITED FH

My mother had her first stroke at the age of 42 and

subsequently died from a second stroke. Several people in my mother's family suffered from high blood cholesterol. The odds were fifty-fifty that I would inherit a gene for familial hypercholesterolaemia. What this means is that I inherited a defective system for the removal of cholesterol from the body – and high blood cholesterol causes coronary heart disease.

HOW MANY PEOPLE DOES THIS AFFECT?

One in every 500 persons inherits this gene and has FH – and most of them don't know they have it. Therefore, they are not doing anything to control it. Those of us who have FH are certainly at risk.

Cholesterol is one of the fatty substances found in the blood and in all body tissues. High blood cholesterol means an amount of cholesterol in the blood which is higher than normal. 200 mg per decilitre is the agreed optimal level of serum cholesterol. If higher the doctor should measure high density lipoprotein and low density lipoprotein levels and advise the patient to be aware of a healthy diet and exercise. People with high blood cholesterol tend to have a greater risk of developing coronary heart disease. Coronary heart disease is a narrowing of the coronary arteries which convey blood to the heart. The narrowing is caused by a build-up of fatty cholesterol deposits. There are many different causes for high blood lipids and people with hypercholesterolaemia may not have FH.

HOW DO I FIND OUT IF I HAVE FH – ARE THERE ANY VISIBLE SYMPTOMS?

Your family G.P. can ask you some questions about your family history, check for certain physical symptoms that people with FH have and, by taking a blood test, check the amount of cholesterol in the blood.

As between one third to one half of all British people die of heart disease many people will have a history of this in their family, but specific information about your parents, brothers, sisters, grandparents, uncles and aunts, will give a good indication if there is a risk of your having inherited FH. Normally there are no outward signs of developing CHD but people with inherited FH may have certain indications such as:

Bumps or swelling in the tendons on the back of the hands, elbows, buttocks, knees or ankles as a result of cholesterol build-up there. These are called xanthomas.

A white band toward the edge of the iris (the coloured part of the eye) evident in people under 40. This is a corneal arcus.

Yellow lumps or streaks of fat in the skin close to the eye, known as xanthelasmas.

However, outward signs of FH are not present in all patients and a blood test will give the doctor conclusive information. So if a close relative had a heart attack or stroke at a young age (under 55) or if someone in your family has high blood cholesterol, you should consult your family doctor.

HOW OLD MUST YOU BE BEFORE FH CAN BE DETECTED?

FH can be detected by a blood test at any age after a child's first birthday, or even earlier. It is wise to test a child's blood for cholesterol if one of the parents finds out that they are affected. The chances are fifty-fifty that a child would have inherited it, but it is essential that your doctor should check the child. If a person is tested, no matter how young, and shown not to have FH, there is no need to worry further as it will not develop later, though of course the person may still be in danger from other risk factors.

WHAT DO I DO IF I HAVE FH?

People with inherited FH have a higher risk of developing

CHD than the average person, but, as we will see throughout the book, both types of coronary heart disease can be controlled and prevented and, as it is a progressive disease, the sooner you do something about it the better. When it is discovered that a child has inherited FH, the treatment can begin at once, thereby lessening the chance of CHD ever developing. It can be controlled by a change in diet and with drug therapy. A self-help group for patients with FH will give you further information if you need it. Write to:

> The Hon Secretary
> FH Association
> PO Box 612, LONDON W2 2EE

HOW SERIOUS IS IT IF FH REMAINS UNDETECTED OR IF I DECIDE NOT TO CONSULT MY DOCTOR EVEN IF I FEEL FH MAY BE IN THE FAMILY?

The outlook for someone with FH is more serious than for someone who has raised blood cholesterol for other reasons. On average 50 per cent of men with this condition will have had a heart attack by the age of 50 and about half of those will probably have died. As explained already, if you have inherited FH, there is a chance your children could inherit it also. Therefore the sooner children develop better diets and lifestyle, the sooner it is controlled.

SMOKING

'With cigarette smoking we feel the answers are now known. There is no doubt that cigarette smoking increases one's risk of heart disease . . . the more one smokes the greater the risk . . . on stopping smoking, the increased risk decreases rapidly. In about one year it is only some 10 per cent above that of the non-smoker and over about a 10 year period it falls to the normal range. Thus we vigorously and aggressively advocate smoking cessation.'

Dr R. I. Levy, National Heart and Lung Institute, USA, 1979.

At least 50 million Americans and approximately sixteen million British people smoke cigarettes regularly. Although cigarette smoking has diminished over the past ten years, the number of girls who start smoking as teenagers has continued to rise. The campaign against cigarette smoking and the resulting cancer continues, but out of the 100,000 premature deaths from cigarette smoking each year in the UK, one in five is due to lung cancer. More than one in three is due to coronary heart disease.

DOESN'T SMOKING CIGARETTES WITH FILTER TIPS AND LOWER TAR HELP?

There has been a slight decrease in lung cancer mortality, but not in the incidence of death from CHD.

HOW DOES SMOKING AFFECT YOUR HEART?

Two main effects of smoking further the development of CHD; the effect of nicotine and carbon monoxide. Nicotine increases the amount of adrenaline into the bloodstream, thereby increasing the heart rate and raising blood pressure, and therefore increasing the demand for oxygen by the heart. It is also responsible for irregular heartbeat (ventricular arrhythmias). Quite simply it makes your heart work harder. Nicotine also affects the release of blood lipids (cholesterol and triglycerides) into the bloodstream, which raise the level of cholesterol and other fats in the blood. Nicotine also increases the stickiness of blood platelets which may cause clots and encourage build-up on the walls of arteries.

The carbon monoxide content of cigarette smoke is very high. It combines with haemoglobin more readily than with oxygen and as it disassociates very slowly, it competes with oxygen to be carried to the blood thereby reducing the amount of oxygen carried to the heart and the brain. This happens when cigarette smoke is inhaled. If there is a narrowing of the arteries and blood flow to the heart is restricted, any decrease in the amount of oxygen in this blood is very dangerous. When nicotine and carbon monoxide work together in cigarette smoke the risk of a heart attack is increased. The nicotine causes a rise in blood pressure and a faster heart beat which means that the heart is working harder and needs more oxygen. The carbon monoxide also displaces the oxygen in the blood by almost 20 per cent, causing the heart to work harder to get oxygen. Both increase the tendency to ventricular fibrillation and to clotting of the blood, which all increase the risk of the series of events that lead to a heart attack.

Smoking 20 cigarettes a day increases the risk of dying from CHD before the age of 50 by three times. There is no 'safe level of smoking'. Both carbon monoxide and nicotine have a harmful effect on the cardiovascular system, which may be critical for persons with CHD – whether they know they have it or not. People with CHD should avoid the smoke from others. It is bad, for instance, to be in a pub or crowded room inhaling the smoke from other people's cigarettes.

HIGH BLOOD PRESSURE OR HYPERTENSION

Of all the risk factors for cardiovascular disease, hypertension has received the greatest attention over the past fifteen years. It is easy to detect and can easily be brought under control and the risk removed.

WHAT IS HIGH BLOOD PRESSURE?

There are two readings a doctor takes when he checks your blood pressure – systolic and diastolic. Both readings are concerned with the left ventricle of the heart. When the left ventricle contracts and propels blood into the arteries, your systolic pressure can be measured – when the force of the contraction increases, the pressure increases. If your arteries are narrow (as they are in CHD) more pressure is needed to pump blood through these narrowed arteries. When the left ventricle relaxes and refills with blood in preparation for its next beat, the diastolic pressure is the pressure in the arterial system needed to pump the blood into the left ventricle. If the muscles in the walls of the blood vessels are elastic and healthy, less pressure is needed to pump the necessary blood – if the arteries are narrowed or if the walls have lost some elasticity, the diastolic pressure will be higher.

WHAT SHOULD I DO IF I HAVE HIGH BLOOD PRESSURE?

If your blood pressure is found to be high your doctor may decide that you need to lose weight, stop smoking and reduce stress. He will probably ask you to reduce the amount of salt and fats in your diet. He may also choose to give you a drug which will effectively reduce blood pressure without unpleasant side-effects. High blood pressure can be controlled through diet and drugs.

IS HIGH BLOOD PRESSURE DANGEROUS?

Untreated high blood pressure is a strong risk factor for some serious illnesses; such as heart attack, stroke, kidney disease, eye disease.

HOW DOES HIGH BLOOD PRESSURE INCREASE THE RISK OF HEART DISEASE?

High blood pressure seems to accelerate the development of atherosclerosis leading to structural changes in the arteries. The higher the pressure the greater the amount of vascular damage, and the higher the chance of a heart attack. Even a mild elevation is dangerous if not treated and controlled.

WHAT CAUSES HIGH BLOOD PRESSURE?

The specific causes are unknown but a high sodium (salt) intake, obesity, heavy drinking and stress are the likely causes.

CAN IT BE INHERITED?

Yes. Those with hypertensive parents have about twice the likelihood of developing high blood pressure. However this can be recognised very early in life by a doctor.

ARE THERE CERTAIN GEOGRAPHICAL DIFFERENCES IN INCIDENCE OF HYPERTENSION?

Yes, it varies from one country to another. It is a frequent cause of death in Japan yet it is virtually unknown in other areas of the Pacific. In the United States, it is a common disease among blacks in northern cities but seldom occurs in Africa among blacks. It occurs frequently in most of the Western world where diet is suspect.

HIGH BLOOD CHOLESTEROL

'Heart disease is the biggest single male killer in Britain. It is responsible for a quarter of all deaths in England and Wales and 33 per cent in Scotland. *Daily Telegraph*, January 20, 1984.

'Research by the National Heart, Lung and Blood Institute showing what scientists say is the first conclusive evidence that lower cholesterol levels in the bloodstream reduce the rate of heart attacks and coronary heart disease, is being hailed as a 'landmark' study. *New York Times Service*, January 14, 1984

'Big changes in the British diet are needed to prevent thousands of unnecessary early deaths from heart disease, strokes and some cancers.' *National Advisory Committee on Nutrition Education*

In the mid-1950s the 'diet/heart hypothesis' was born in the United States. Deaths from heart disease were said to be due to an excess of saturated fats in the diet. Deaths could therefore be reduced by persuading people to eat less saturated fat. Over the next 30 years health-conscious people and governments in North America and Western Europe encouraged people to eat less fat and to replace dairy fat with acceptable fish and vegetable oils – especially with those high in polyunsaturated fats. The result is that heart disease has been reduced by over 25 per cent in those countries that did something about reducing high cholesterol in the diet. These include the United States, Canada, Australia, Netherlands, Belgium. Evidence linking dietary fat with breast, bowel and colon cancer was persuasive too and this increased the pressure to reduce the level of cholesterol in the blood.

In January 1984, the results of a clinical trial run by America's National Heart, Lung and Blood Institute (NHLBI) were published. In a group of 3,806 middle-aged men with abnormally high levels of cholesterol, half were given cholestyramine, and the other half (the control group) were given a placebo and tests taken for nine years. Among those taking cholestyramine there were 24 per cent fewer fatal heart attacks than among those taking the placebo and 19 per cent fewer non-fatal heart attacks. The treated group showed 20 per cent less angina and a 21 per cent lower need for coronary by-pass surgery. The directors at the US National Institute of Health have claimed that this study conclusively links eating animal fats, high blood cholesterol levels and subsequent heart disease and that the risk of coronary heart disease can be reduced by lowering the level of cholesterol in the blood. This study used cholestyramine to reduce cholesterol levels but it was felt that lowering of cholesterol by dietary means would also be beneficial. Although the study was limited to 'middle-aged men with high cholesterol' the scientists felt that women and younger people could also reduce the risk of heart attacks by lowering cholesterol.

There are doctors who feel that this study was not as conclusive as it claimed to be and they questioned whether or not the general population would benefit from cutting down on their cholesterol. Is reducing the cholesterol by dietary means effective to reduce the level in the blood? Is this only effective for middle-aged men at high risk?

As in all clinical studies there are doctors who will argue both for and against the results, but as a person who had the disease I would like to see more immediate action to *save lives* based upon the vast amount of research that favours the lowering of risk factors to avoid a heart attack. Academic discussions can go on at seminars and papers can be written about all the fine points of the subject, but I feel that our immediate problem is to encourage good health and good diet in all the population, especially those at high risk like myself, as it has been proven in other countries that this approach works in lowering the incidence of heart attacks in the 'entire' population.

WHAT IS CHOLESTEROL?

Cholesterol is a waxy organic, chemical substance. It is manufactured by the body in the liver and is an essential part of cell membranes, and is essential in the making of steroid hormones as well as the male and female sex hormones. But it is also the main component of the fatty deposits called atheroma in the lining of arteries. Cholesterol narrows arteries and may block the flow of blood to the heart. It causes heart attacks and strokes. *Cholesterol can kill you.*

Cholesterol is transported in the bloodstream through the body, to the vital organs. We can measure the amount of cholesterol and other fatty substances with a blood test. The average level of blood cholesterol is 220 mg/dl (Milligrams per decilitre). Over 220 requires medical attention.

Some people have livers that produce too much cholesterol and their bodies fail to re-absorb or eliminate the excess efficiently. Although most of the cholesterol is produced in the liver, 20 to 30 per cent comes from the food we eat – the dietary source of cholesterol. If we eat excessive amounts of food rich in cholesterol, it may attach itself to the linings of the coronary arteries – and this causes coronary heart disease. This condition occurs in people who have a combination of risk factors (including high blood cholesterol) that will gradually cause the development of this disease.

WHAT CAUSES HIGH BLOOD CHOLESTEROL?

The condition may be inherited but it is normally caused by a diet with a high level of foods containing saturated fat. We have heard so much about this subject – what is good for us and what is bad – that I feel the scientific explanation is the best way to approach the subject of dietary fat.

There are two types of cholesterol. Dietary cholesterol from the food we eat and bile cholesterol which is found in the gastro-intestinal tract. Dietary saturated fat raises the level of cholesterol in the blood. Major sources of saturated fatty acids are meat fats; dairy fats present in products such as whole milk, cream, butter, cheese and ice-cream; commercial baked goods; and the fats used for spreads, salads and cooking (i.e. butter, lard, hard margarine and shortenings; cheese-based dressings for salads). Egg yolk is a rich source of cholesterol.

52

Monounsaturated fats neither raise nor lower the concentration of cholesterol. Fat from poultry is less saturated than that from red meats. Fish tends to be high in polyunsaturated fatty acids.

Polyunsaturated fats are found in many (but not all) vegetable oils, including corn, soybean, safflower, and sunflower oils. These are high in linoleic acids, and have the effect of lowering the level of cholesterol in the blood – *2 grams of polyunsaturated fat in the diet removes 1 gram of saturated fat.*

As in all other risk factors, high blood cholesterol acts in combination with the other risks to cause CHD. So a diet high in cholesterol combined with little physical exercise, high alcohol consumption, cigarette smoking and high blood pressure, will increase the risk of heart attack considerably.

IF YOU HAVE A HIGH LEVEL OF CHOLESTEROL CAN IT BE LOWERED?

Yes. As the president of the American Heart Association Antonio M. Gotto MD, stated,

> 'A prudent diet will lower cholesterol, on average about ten to fifteen per cent – enough to benefit a person with borderline cholesterol elevations. But, of course, I agree that it would be far better to lower cholesterol by 30 to 40 per cent, but to do that, one must usually resort to drugs. You simply cannot reduce cholesterol to that extent with diet alone in most patients.'
> *Modern Medicine* 1981, 49(13): 90–108.

The dietary intake of cholesterol from foods high in saturated fats can be controlled by eating less fats or by substituting polyunsaturated fats for the saturated fats (see page 128). This means that you will reduce the amount of fats, including cholesterol, that enter your body. The body

53

already manufactures its own cholesterol and sometimes it produces more than is needed. In these cases diet may not be enough to reduce the level sufficiently. Other lifestyle changes may be needed, such as weight reduction and more exercise.

Cholesterol is produced by the liver and enters the gastro-intestinal tract where bile acids then cause it either to be re-absorbed into the body, or excreted.* A drug can be prescribed to act on the liver to control this overproduction of cholesterol, or a 'resin-sequestrant', cholestyramine, will be prescribed to absorb or sponge up the bile acids before being transported back to the liver to be reprocessed into the body, passed into the colon and excreted from the body.

Each case has different factors that determine what treatment is necessary, and only your doctor or a lipid consultant can make that decision.

WHAT HAPPENS ONCE YOU HAVE NARROWED ARTERIES?

If the disease has progressed to the point where the narrowing of the arteries presents an immediate danger, surgery may be the answer. There have been enormous advances in bypass surgery and in other methods in the past ten years (see Surgery, page 76). But doctors have proven that regression (reversal) is possible and may occur when the cholesterol level is brought down to normal through diet and drug therapy. Of course, other risk factors must be minimised as well.

WHAT ARE TRIGLYCERIDES AND LIPOPROTEINS?

Cholesterol is one of the fatty or lipid substances in the

---

* Bile salts normally circulate several cycles before they are excreted in faeces.

blood along with phospholipids, triglycerides, and fatty acids. These don't exist in a free form in the bloodstream – they form complexes with proteins and are carried as lipoproteins. LDL or low density lipoproteins carry $\frac{1}{2}$ to $\frac{2}{3}$ of cholesterol in the blood. This helps to deposit cholesterol in the arterial wall and leads to development of atherosclerotic plaque. LDL is 'bad'. HDL or high density lipoproteins are considered to be protective in the blood and help to lower the cholesterol level. The other lipoproteins are VLDL or very low density lipoproteins (which account for the majority of plasma triglycerides) and chylomicrons. The latter carry dietary cholesterol and triglycerides (or blood fat) which numbers rise rapidly after a fat-containing meal. A high concentration of triglycerides in the blood is not good, as triglycerides are associated with increased risk.

PHYSICAL INACTIVITY – LACK OF EXERCISE

Modern technology and lifestyle have changed the type and amount of exercise we undertake. Until this century people engaged in vigorous activity in their normal work, home and leisure lives. Passive pursuits such as watching television and spectator sports have replaced active physical participation and very few people are truly physically fit. The recent surge in interest in exercise and fitness in the United States has resulted in half the American adult population engaging in regular exercise or sport activity. This is about twice as many reported exercising in 1960.

FACT:
Vigorous physical activity reduces the risk of CHD. Moderately intense activities, such as walking, dancing cycling, swimming, gardening, and climbing stairs have been found to be significantly associated with lower risk of coronary disease.

HOW DOES EXERCISE REDUCE THE RISK OF CORONARY HEART DISEASE?

There is evidence that aerobic exercise (moderately intensive exercise done at a steady pace for about 20 minutes, three times a week) has a protective effect by reducing other CHD risk factors;

1. *Obesity* – Physically active people are usually thinner than inactive people. Exercise reduces body weight, increases use of energy, raises the rate of metabolism, burns up body fat, influences appetite and eating patterns. A loss of weight along with changes in diet may alter other coronary risk factors favourably, including blood pressure, blood lipid profile and glucose tolerance. (Glucose or dextrose is a simple sugar whose concentration in the blood either above or below the normal level can cause illness, including diabetes.)

2. *High blood pressure* – Exercise lowers blood pressure by dilating small blood vessels in muscles and skin.

3. *Blood lipids* – Exercise seems to increase high density lipoproteins and causes a decrease in low density lipoproteins.

4. *Insulin and glucose tolerance* – Exercise has a beneficial effect on glucose metabolism, blood insulin levels and diabetic control.

5. *Other health habits* – Regular exercise favourably alters poor health habits such as smoking, excessive alcohol consumption, and overeating.

THAT MID-AFTERNOON LET-DOWN

When you feel that urge to grab a biscuit or a bar of chocolate, eat a pastry, light up a cigarette or drink a cup of coffee, your body is asking you for a lift. It wants a 'burst of energy' from instant blood sugar. One way to respond is to add fuel in the form of calories and sugar – instant but not nutritious.

The other way is from a short burst of exercise to convert fats into blood sugar, raising your metabolic rate and doubling your body's intake of oxygen and pumping your blood through your veins. It will wake you up and renew your lost energy. Jumping up and down on the spot or an exercise bicycle or a brisk walk will do the trick. I realise that this isn't practical all the time, but remember that exercise is an alternative to the 'quick energy or stress fix' – the cigarette, coffee, soft drinks and chocolate.

OBESITY

We all know that being overweight is bad for us. At birth the human body contains twelve per cent fat; at ten years, eighteen per cent; at puberty there is a significant increase in the percentage of fat in females – in males a small, significant drop in body fat (at age eighteen, males have fifteen to eighteen per cent; females have 20 to 25 per cent). Between the ages of 20 to 50 the fat content of males doubles, and that of females increases to 50 per cent of body weight. The increased fat is due to the rise in body weight and in part due to a reduction in a lean body mass.

'Almost 40 per cent of British men and 32 per cent of women are overweight'. Office of Population Censuses and Surveys. DHSS report, Heights and Weights of Adults in Great Britain.

HOW DOES BEING OVERWEIGHT AFFECT YOUR BODY?

Excess weight is associated with an increased mortality rate, which may include hypertension, gall bladder disease and diabetes.

1. Obesity increases the workload of the heart – output,

stroke volume and blood volume all increase.

2. Blood pressure rises.

3. Obesity increases the level of cholesterol in the blood (lowers high density lipoproteins and increases lower density lipoproteins).

4. Obesity adversely affects lung function (increases hyperventilation).

5. Endocrine function is modified, plasma insulin is increased and glucose tolerance is impaired. Obesity increases demand on the pancreas and may lead to development of clinical diabetes.

6. Obesity impairs release of growth hormone from the pituitary gland.

HOW DO I KNOW IF I AM OVERWEIGHT?

Life assurance companies express overweight as a percentage of average weight for the individual's height and age. Your chances of living a normal life span decrease by fifteen per cent with each ten per cent increase in weight. The most direct effect of obesity is on blood pressure, that is, an increase in weight and rise in blood pressure often run parallel.

(British Heart Foundation booklet No 7.)

STRESS AND PERSONALITY TYPE

It is very difficult to measure the exact effect of stress on coronary heart disease. We all know how a stressful situation makes the pulse race. Emotional stress, or physical exertion can elevate our blood pressure and cause our hearts to beat rapidly.

DOES STRESS INCREASE THE RISK OF CHD?

Prolonged stress will alter the body chemistry, releasing

hormones that can harm the body. Stress may lead us to increase the risk factors that are a direct cause of CHD, smoking, drinking to excess or eating foods that are chemically bad for the system but which seem to relax and pacify us. Emotional stress at home or at work may lead to behavioural problems that eventually become medical problems.

IS STRESS INHERITED?

We are all born with certain drives for survival and success, and some of us have temperaments better suited to deal with stressful situations. Freud and Adler claimed that self-preservation along with a drive for economic security were our principal drives. And once we achieve the success the need for personal recognition and friendships becomes important. There is in all of us a fear of failure and rejection which may cause feelings of guilt and complexes to develop.

HOW DOES THE BODY REACT TO STRESS?

In times of stress, either physical or emotional, the involuntary nervous system will release adrenaline and noradrenaline which will vary in proportion to the amount of stress we experience in each situation. This surge of hormones will release fatty acids into the blood to provide an instant source of energy to cope with the situation. Blood pressure rises under stress and blood clotting time is shortened. The heart under stress will demand more oxygen and will be forced to work harder. All these reactions may increase the chance of CHD. Emotional changes under stress will affect the nervous system which regulates the heart beat and can cause arrhythmias (rapid and irregular heartbeat) and sudden death.

CAN YOU LEARN TO COPE WITH STRESS?

A combination of stress and personality traits can lead to a 'pre-coronary syndrome' – pressure at work and home begin to build up and can get on top of the person both mentally and physically. This cycle, if not stopped, may lead to CHD and a heart attack or stroke. .

Something *can* be done about it which will include reducing some of the risk factors that this stressful period probably increased, such as smoking, heavy drinking and bad eating habits.

IF YOU ARE UNDER STRESS WILL YOU HAVE A HEART ATTACK?

Physical or mental exhaustion, a feeling of emotional drain and a sudden tiredness, weariness and fatigue can be early warning signals for a heart attack. There is increasing information that shows physical exhaustion to be a symptom that can appear from as little as a few days to as much as a month before a heart attack. Fatigue seems to be a more common symptom than chest pain. Stress hormones can cause arterial spasms and a tendency for the blood to clot more quickly than normal (see page 84) which may cause sudden death.

ARE SOME OF US MORE AT RISK THAN OTHERS?

Yes, Dr Ray Rosenman and Dr Meyer Friedman in their book *Type A behaviour and Your Heart* explained that intense behavioural patterns are found in people with an identifiable style of life. They are called Type A and some doctors feel that they are more likely to develop CHD than Type B people.

WHAT IS TYPE A BEHAVIOUR?

As stated by Rosenman, Friedman and others, Type A behaviour pattern may be recognised by some or all of the following characteristics: competitiveness, intense drive, ambition, easily provoked to anger and hostility, an overly aggressive attitude, fierce determination to get things done, always in a hurry, punctuality is a rule, extreme impatience, always racing against time, an exterior of control and politeness but appears to be strained. A Type A personality has abrupt and rapid speech and gestures, may sacrifice other parts of life to attain self-selected goals, and sometimes doesn't communicate with others. He is overcommitted to work and professional achievement at the expense of other aspects of life – including his family life. He is never off work sick, won't go to a doctor, refuses to go to bed early, devotes little time to home life and decision-making in the home, rarely exercises, combines holidays with business, works late at the office, makes snap decisions, has no creative activities, smokes cigarettes, holds his hands slightly clenched – tension can be seen through his body language and gestures. He may hum, whistle, twitch his leg nervously.

WHAT IS TYPE B BEHAVIOUR?

Type B people behave in quite the opposite way. They are: calmer, unhurried, less preoccupied with achievement, lack a competitive attitude, do not react aggressively, and have a more relaxed speech and gesture pattern.

Occupations involving higher levels of prestige and higher education tend to have higher proportions of Type A persons. Top executives and executive secretaries are more usually Type A – and are two or three times more likely to have a heart attack and develop CHD in middle age.

AGEING

DO MEN AND WOMEN HAVE THE SAME RISK OF CHD?

Mortality from CHD is related to age in each sex. 'Although uncommon in young white women CHD is already a major cause of death for men aged 35 to 44 years. By ages 55 to 64, 40 per cent of all deaths among men are due to this single cause. The male predominance in CHD mortality applies in both whites and non-whites.' (However, it is more prevalent in younger whites. Females are affected much later in life – ten years for whites and seven for non-whites.) 'CHD is still a very common disease in women and their leading cause of deaths.

An escalation of CHD incidence and a dramatic increase in the severity of the disease are noted in women after menopause. Women in their 40s and 50s who underwent menopause were found to have more than double the incidence of CHD of women the same age who remained premenopausal.' William B. Kannel in *Prevention of Coronary Heart Disease*, Kaplan and Stamler, W. B. Sanders Company, 1983.

American white males under 45 are ten times more likely to develop CHD than women.

In people 45 to 54 years old, the difference in CHD risk is explained by the greater risk factor levels in men. The cholesterol level (lower density lipoprotein) is lower in women before age 50, but higher after that age.

WHY ARE WOMEN MORE AT RISK AFTER MENOPAUSE?

One view states that the logical factor for the change in risk after menopause is simply the decrease in oestrogen levels. Oestrogen seems to protect women against CHD and heart attacks. Yet clinical trials ended in disagreement about the success of oestrogen therapy to prevent heart attacks after menopause. In fact, concerning CHD, some doctors claim postmenopausal women taking hormones have a double risk. (W. B. Kannel. *Prevention of CHD* Kaplan & Stamler, W. B. Sanders Company, 1983.) The factors responsible for the change in risk in women after menopause have not yet been defined.

There is support for the claim that oestrogens in oral contraceptives may promote the development of coronary disease. In healthy women under 45, the risk estimate for oral contraceptive users was $4\frac{1}{2}$ times higher when compared with that of non-users. Studies have found that cigarette smokers above the age of 35 are most prone to heart attacks, therefore the risk for non-smoking oral contraceptive users is much smaller. (Kaplan and Stamler p. 143).

LIVING WITH ALCOHOL

The evidence damning excessive alcohol consumption is enormous. Excessive drinking is second only to smoking as the cause of preventable deaths. There are five to seventeen million alcoholics in the United States and almost a million in Britain. At least a third of drivers and a quarter of pedestrians killed in road accidents have had blood alcohol levels over the legal limit. This is the chief cause of premature deaths in younger people. Deaths from cirrhosis of the liver have increased more than 60 per cent in Great Britain. Drinking is associated with suicide, industrial accidents, sex crimes, robberies and murders. It increases the risk of cancer of the liver, mouth, tongue and oesophagus. Consumption of large amounts of alcohol increases CHD mortality. It causes damage to the brain and nervous system as well as personal and social harm.

HOW MUCH IS SAFE?

The Health Education Council considers 20 units of alcohol a week (three a day) for men and thirteen for women to be safe, moderate drinking levels. The unit is a glass of wine, or a single measure of spirits or a half pint of beer.

Alcohol in quantity will increase the amount of fats in the blood and will weaken the heart muscle. It raises the triglyceride concentration by delaying the clearing of fats from the blood.

Alcohol has adverse effects on the liver and virtually all tissues in the body including heart and arteries.

FACT:
Alcohol abuse can lead to a full-blown hyperlipidemia, may affect triglyceride levels, raise uric acid levels and elevate enzymes related to liver functions.

Alcoholic drinks are fattening and high in calories – beer, cocktails, mixed drinks have a high sugar content. A drinker's environment is not a spartan one and other temptations are present such as cigarette smoking, potato crisps, nuts, and so on. He or she is more likely to meet people with the same social and personal stresses and with them exercise is not a priority. As CHD is caused by an excess of risk factors interacting to cause a problem, moderate to heavy drinking seems to breed excess in many of the risk areas. It is significant that in parts of Great Britain where heart disease is at its peak, such as Scotland, heavy drinking and alcoholism is also a major social problem.

However, in contrast to the confirmed facts about heavy drinking and heart disease, evidence has been accumulated that raises the possibility that alcohol, consumed daily in small to moderate amounts, reduces risk of coronary heart disease. This presents a separate issue. The excess drinkers must cut down on their alcohol consumption just as overweight people must eat less. The chance that light drinking might lower blood fats should not act as a spur to start people drinking or to encourage one to drink more; it would then be counterproductive. This just reinforces my attitude that things in moderation will give you a better lifestyle. The theory postulates that moderate consumption of alcohol inhibits atherosclerosis, lowers blood pressure, keeps blood from clotting, and removes stress from Type A personalities. No medical conclusions may yet be drawn.

HOW DO I KNOW IF I AM AT RISK?

You are now aware of the various risk factors that contribute to the development of CHD. See how many of them apply to you. The more you have, the more at risk you are. Even if you are not at risk of CHD, you should minimise the risk factors and become aware of your general health and how to live a healthier life. It's your body – you must learn to take care of it.

CAN I LOOK FOR SOME SIGNS ON MY BODY?

Other than the signs found in patients with FH the first sign of CHD is usually a heart attack – that is because most of us are not aware of how much our way of living, eating and playing affects our heart and arteries. Now that you are familiar with the risk factors, a good look at yourself and an examination of your lifestyle (the truth, not through rose-coloured glasses) will give you a fair estimate of whether you are at risk.

You should know:

1. if you are overweight
2. if you smoke too much
3. if you eat the wrong foods, or are you unaware of what is good and bad for you?
4. if you drink excessively
5. if you are a Type A personality
6. if you have a family history of CHD

Once you have determined whether you feel you may be at risk, the only person who can tell you the scientific facts is your doctor. He can take your blood pressure, analyse your family history and take a blood sample to determine your blood fats and cholesterol levels.

Worrying will only increase the risk. If you think you are at risk you should see your doctor, if only to ease your mind. Unfortunately not all doctors are as aware of the recent studies as they should be – therefore you should see a doctor who is aware of the causes of CHD and who also practises preventive medicine – that is, one who doesn't prescribe something after it happens but who sees it coming and will do something to keep you out of hospital, rather than waiting until you get sick and then admitting you. It is true that the NHS is overworked but as we now know the causes of CHD and how to treat it, the person at risk should be treated as early as possible. If you feel you have reason to suspect you are at risk, you must insist that your blood cholesterol levels be checked.

As I already mentioned, chest pains may be a symptom of angina or heart disease, therefore a chest pain from the heart muscle reaching up into the neck, down the left arm – sometimes choking and gripping in nature – is reason for you to see your doctor immediately. Even if it goes away, once is enough! See your doctor! Don't be afraid of causing a problem or being thought a hypochondriac. The alternative may be death.

Chest pain may be caused by something quite unrelated to CHD, such as, indigestion, shingles, fibrositis, arthritis, stomach ulcers, hernia, pleurisy or pneumonia. If your doctor is unsure of the cause of your pain he will refer you to a consultant.

COPING WITH YOUR RISK FACTORS

So you think you've got it . . . What do you do now?

After reading about risk factors I hope you are now aware of what causes CHD and whether you are a person potentially or currently at risk. If you feel that I have been talking about *you*, don't worry, because most of us, on reading an article about the symptoms of a disease, immediately feel we've got it! That's one of the reasons why it is very important to have a doctor you respect and trust – as only he (or she) must be the one to take the first steps to diagnosing whether or not you have CHD. But it is your analysis that determines if you visit your doctor or not. Remember CHD doesn't have any symptoms in its early stages – so even if you feel good you may still be developing this progressive disease.

DIAGNOSTIC MEDICINE

Once you are concerned about your risks and a logical analysis seems to show you might have CHD (family history, Type A personality, bad diet), go and see your doctor. Questions and a brief examination will give him much of the information he needs about the state of your heart, and he will take your blood pressure and arrange for a blood sample to be tested. The blood test is the only thing that will tell him the level of your blood lipids (fats), which is the clue to CHD.

ELECTROCARDIOGRAM

He also might want to take an electrocardiogram (ECG). This test is painless and is usually done in the outpatient department of your local hospital, or your doctor may have the machine in his surgery. A series of electrodes are put onto the skin to monitor your heartbeat from different points of the body. It will show any abnormal heart rhythms and pinpoint where they come from. It will indicate if you have suffered a mild heart attack in the past (some heart attacks and angina are slight and may not have been noticed when they occurred) and will also detect any thickening of the heart muscle not yet detectable clinically. It will also show any undue reaction to stress.

The limitation of the electrocardiogram is that it reflects what has happened in the past, and if you have symptomless coronary disease or angina, your trace may be normal.

As more and more is learned about the causes and the treatments for coronary heart disease, the one area that is still a problem is the diagnostic stage. Without symptoms it is difficult to detect the disease. But research is beginning to produce results.

EXERCISE STRESS TEST

Variations on this ECG, taken during exercise, can prove much more. A stress test is carried out on an exercise bicycle or an exercise treadmill. The object is to see your heart's reaction to stress and exercise. When you exercise your heart pumps more blood to meet its increased requirement for oxygen. A healthy heart will meet this demand, but if the person has narrowed arteries, the heart will not be able to supply the oxygen required and therefore will pump less efficiently. If a test is given under these increased stress conditions it may be possible to detect abnormal heart functions that are not detectable in a resting patient. It is about 70 per cent accurate in detecting latent heart disease, but it will only monitor abnormalities that show up at the moment of the test. This test will carefully and gradually exercise your heart to 50 to 70 per cent of its capacity, and, theoretically, if your heart has any weakness it will show up electrically on the machine. As our health and physical well-being varies from day to day, a stress test may exercise you to 65 per cent and your abnormality may not show up until 67 per cent. It is not foolproof but will give your doctor further evidence about the state of your heart, this time under stress, rather than at rest in his office.

Excessive exercise or stress on your heart can produce a heart attack if you are not fit, even in a stress test. Therefore, don't try to check your fitness yourself by racing frantically on a friend's exercise cycle or dashing around a track checking your pulse rate – it is a job for experts. A stress test as well as other tests to diagnose heart disease should be carried out under careful and experienced medical supervision, preferably by a cardiologist, to be safe.

ANGIOGRAM (Cardiac catheterisation)

When I visited Dr Rickards, he felt that he needed to know more about the state of my coronary arteries as I had a family history of CHD as well as a personal history and, at that time, chest pain. He decided that an angiogram would give him the information he needed to diagnose properly the extent of the damage done to my arteries. Doctors are very cautious about invasive tests. 'Invasive' tests are those which involve surgery or those in which an instrument is inserted into your body to diagnose an illness, (rather than the doctor listening to your heart, taking blood pressure or first taking a blood sample). An angiogram is a test that is given by inserting a tube-like needle (called a catheter) into the arm or the leg and passing it up through to the arterial system into the heart. A dye is inserted into the catheter and pumped by the heart into the coronary arteries. Sophisticated methods are used to film the arteries at work. The dye reveals the extent of the narrowing within each of the coronary arteries. This is extremely accurate, and gives the doctor a picture of the real situation within the arteries and the heart. But as this process involves 'surgery' it does have an element of risk. There is a small possibility that the test might induce a heart attack or trigger some abnormality to react to the techniques. Therefore it is usually done if a person is thought to need a bypass (see page 76) or heart surgery and accurate information is needed by the surgeon to assess the extent of the condition.

The test itself is relatively painless, but can be frightening. The unknown is often frightening. I think, however, I was more worried about the results of the test, than the test itself. In my case the truth was encouraging and my doctor knew the exact state of my arteries. There was no need for any of my arteries to be replaced, and instead diet, exercise and medicines were prescribed. I was glad I had had the test because it meant all the guesswork was over, and with CHD it is important to have as full a picture of the illness as possible.

I have no fear of having an angiogram again – the only unnerving feeling is that of being in hospital and surrounded by the people and machines that are necessary. We all have those fears, but the peace of mind that results from knowing the truth is worth it.

WHAT'S IN THE PIPELINE?

A foolproof, less invasive form of diagnosis is what is needed – the less the test interferes with the body, the better. A form of *nuclear scanning* may be one of the answers. In this case radioisotopes (radioactive substances that give off radiation to trace the inside of the body) are injected into the bloodstream until they reach the heart muscle. The radiation is then scanned by a machine and a computer converts the scan into a picture.

Another scanning system based upon radioactive isotopes is *PET* scanning (Positron Emission Tomography). A shortlived radioactive substance made in a cyclotron (a complex and expensive process) is inhaled by, or injected into the patient. It emits positron particles which are used in body metabolism (chemical changes that take place within the body) and which, when they interact with electrons, emit gamma-rays. Tiny electronic detectors pick up these gamma-rays which are transformed by a computer into an image that looks like a map of the body. This will show blockages in the arteries or heart defects that are not visible through X-ray techniques.

Magnetic Resonance scanning uses pulses of radiowaves and a powerful magnet to produce pictures of the inside of the body. These body scanners are being developed and perfected at a rapid pace and hopefully will help safely to diagnose coronary artery disease.

MEDICINE AND DRUGS – RESEARCH AND OTHER GOOD NEWS

Advancement in the area of drugs has been rapid and there are drugs to treat many of the problems faced by the CHD sufferer.

If your doctor feels that you have CHD, he will attempt to determine how far advanced it is. Those of us with FH are more at risk and we need to approach our treatment very seriously.

I was able to control my cholesterol level simply by diet and weight loss ten years ago, but now I take a twice daily dose of a resin called Questran. For my type of hyperlipidaemia (high blood fats) problem, cholestyramine was the cholesterol-lowering agent selected by my doctor. It acts in the lower intestines by absorbing and eliminating bile salts, and is classified as a bile-sequestering resin, rather than acting on an organ, such as the liver, as drugs do. Cholestyramine, may cause flatulence, nausea or indigestion in some cases.

Medical experts feel that certain drugs have no place in the broad public health effort to prevent CHD by serum lipid reduction. Your doctor or blood lipid consultant is the one to make the decision as to whether you need to take a drug to supplement your lifestyle changes. Cholestyramine, the resin in Questran, is mixed with water. Although some people say that it 'tastes funny', I don't find it any different from a glass of orange juice in the morning. If your doctor prescribes an oral medicine you should be grateful that you don't have diabetes where the alternative is a daily injection of insulin – consider yourself lucky. Remember, if you are told to take a medicine regularly, take it regularly, *don't forget!*

Additional drugs are still under investigation, and your doctor will have information that will allow him to decide what drug you should take.

There have been many studies aimed at lowering cholesterol and stress. Some studies have isolated individuals and supervised their diets and influenced their mental states. These have included low fat diets, vegetarian diets and stress management techniques such as meditation, yoga, visualisation, and other very important and positive methods that do work.

I feel that these 'laboratory conditions' are valid ways of introducing people to what they should be doing ideally, but the dramatic results achieved do not reflect a true lifestyle change that is needed as a daily, workable, effective, long-term answer. These programmes are like crash diets – once you come off them you tend to revert to your past habits and select the isolated exercises or diet changes that you feel are compatible with your existing lifestyle. These studies proved the results of some theoretical methods. The only way we can change an existing pattern of eating and living is through a programme of moderation to be practised by individuals in their own way to suit their existing lifestyles. That is the only way to 'make it stick' in the daily routine and not become a periodic rationalisation for bad habits practised throughout the year. It cannot be a vacation from excess and indulgence.

DRUGS

There are drugs available which control angina and high blood pressure – they have been used for years and are safe – and a visit to your doctor will assure relief if you are suffering from these heart problems.

BETA-BLOCKERS

Drug therapy for heart problems has developed rapidly since the arrival of beta-blockers in 1967. These are the drugs most frequently prescribed, along with the short acting nitrates for effort angina, or heart pain. The types of beta-blockers include propranolol, atenolol, acebutolol, oxprenolol and pindolol. Slow release pills are available so that you can take them once a day rather than the four times a day as formerly prescribed. In addition to offering relief from angina pain they significantly lower the danger of incurring a second heart attack. They act by obstructing the message from the brain to the heart to increase the heart rate. This eases the workload on the heart and also controls an unexplained call from the brain for the heart to increase its rate excessively (as in ventricular fibrillation). As beta-blockers are complex, though effective drugs, they do have some side-effects and cannot be given indiscriminately. They are sometimes prescribed together with another drug and the combination seems to be better tolerated and more effective than the beta-blocker alone.

One beneficial side-effect of beta-blockers is a dramatic lessening of anxiety. Unlike tranquillizers they don't seem to affect concentration. I take a beta-blocker once a day, and I find that it relaxes me in a general way so that problems seem to be reduced slightly by my calmer approach to life. I don't seem to be so on edge. This could be the result of a belief that I am doing something to control my CHD, but I feel that beta-blockers are influencing my control of anxiety, and therefore, stress.

CALCIUM ANTAGONISTS

Calcium antagonists, or calcium channel blockers are very good news. They interfere with calcium ions – the chemical messengers that make the muscles contract, thus allowing the coronary arteries to expand and carry more blood to the heart. At the same time they deprive the heart of calcium which enables it to pump less forcefully. This allows damaged tissue to rebuild and reduces the incidence of arrythmias (any variation from the normal regular heart beat).

ASPIRIN

One of the most exciting developments in recent years is also the simplest. It is now thought that aspirin decreases the body's tendency to produce blood clots and thereby protects against coronary heart disease.

Dr H. Daniel Lewis and his group at the Veterans Administration Medical Center in Kansas City, USA, reported the results of their study:

'This trial demonstrates that a single daily dose of 324 mg of aspirin in buffered solution for 12 weeks has a highly protective effect (51 per cent reduction) against

74

acute myocardial infarction in men with unstable angina. The data also suggests a similar reduction in mortality. There was no evidence of gastrointestinal side effects of aspirin as administered in this trial'.

New England Journal of Medicine, August 18, 1983. Vol 309, No 7

The process of clotting is controlled by chemicals called prostaglandins. One of these, thromboxane A_2, promotes clotting. Aspirin can block its production in the body. Studies have shown that Aspirin can prevent strokes in persons who experience temporary losses of blood flow to the brain and Aspirin is also being used in efforts to prevent strokes and heart attacks in the healthy.

A recent Harvard University study involves giving Aspirin to 10,000 doctors a day over a four year period. It is thought that a single tablet per day on a regular basis will inactivate more than 95 per cent of the platelet enzyme prostaglandin. In the Veterans Administration study quoted above, hospital patients with severe heart pain who took small doses of Aspirin daily for twelve weeks suffered far fewer heart attacks than patients who did not take Aspirin.

CAUTION: Aspirin is a strong drug and should never be over-used. Just because it is a non-prescriptive drug doesn't mean that it should be taken indiscriminately or in excess. Regular use of any drug or medicine should only be taken under a doctor's supervision. Aspirin has strong side-effects, such as promoting internal bleeding, if misused.

Other drugs are currently being tested for their anti-platelet activities.

A heart attack is caused by a clot in a coronary artery. New drugs are being developed to dissolve the clot so that the blood can flow freely. When a blood vessel breaks, blood platelets rush to stop the bleeding, thereby allowing the body to repair the injury. A natural protein, called tissue-type plasminogen activator (TPA) is produced by the body to dissolve 'unwanted' blood clots. Genetic engineering techniques are being used to attempt to produce TPA outside the body. This could dissolve the obstruction and as it is a natural process it would be safe.

For the past few years an enzyme, streptokinase, has been used to unblock vessels to the heart but it has a tendency to promote bleeding and is now injected into the artery, as close as possible to the clot. TPA eats only the clots, is a natural protein and is neutralised in the body quickly. Once in production, an early use of the drug after a heart attack could rapidly restore blood flow to the heart. The blood clot could be dissolved by injecting TPA into a vein, which is a much simpler and safer procedure than injecting streptokinase directly into the blocked artery. Another drug, Warfarin, has been used for some time, but it acts to prevent clotting, not to remove clots after they have formed.

SURGERY

CORONARY BYPASS

Drugs are used to relieve the blockage within the arteries, but in some patients there comes a point where the blockage is so severe that the possibility of further blockage can not be allowed. Bypass operations have been effective and surgeons have altered the techniques to make this operation now a very safe one to perform – but as it involves taking a vein from a patient's leg, grafting one end on to the aorta and the other on to part of the coronary artery beyond the obstruction, it carries some element of risk. This bypass operation creates a detour around the blocked artery. It decreases the risk of heart attacks and restores blood flow.

CORONARY ANGIOPLASTY

Surgeons are trying to develop methods that will unblock the build-up or clot within the artery without having to resort to a bypass.

Coronary angioplasty is one of such methods. A thin tube, a catheter (like the one used for an angiogram) is passed from the arm or groin to the blocked artery. The catheter has a balloon at its tip. The balloon is then inflated within the artery, the fatty obstructions are compressed and blood flow is increased. Coronary angioplasty has removed obstructions in 80 per cent of patients and costs one quarter of the expense of a bypass.

LASER SURGERY

If the blockage is extensive and cannot be compressed through other methods the laserscope may be the answer. It is a new technology using a laser beam carried in optical fibres within a plastic tube. This tube is inserted into the body to the blocked artery. The beam, generated by an argon laser, is extremely accurate and cuts a channel through the atheroma (fatty blockage) to restore blood flow. The technique is complicated – a salt solution is constantly flushed down the plastic tube to stop the blood from absorbing the energy of the laser and prevents the debris from the burning atheroma from collecting inside the artery by 'vacuuming' it.

As it doesn't require the chest to be opened (as in bypass surgery) the shock of laser surgery on the body is much less than with other surgical methods and some people who are too weak to undergo an anaesthetic trauma may be operated on by laser.

PACEMAKERS

A small implant has been developed which, when put into the body and connected to the heart by electrodes. monitors the heart muscle's natural electrical discharge. When an abnormal pattern that indicates a slow heart rate is detected. the unit emits an electrical impulse that will stimulate the heart to correct the arrythmia.

The implants are called pacemakers and are now programmable. They can be regulated by the doctor without surgery. They control heartbeat and are implanted within the patient. The doctor can use a transmitting device to change the pacemaker's strength or rate of pulse.

SOME RISKS YOU MAY NOT HAVE CONSIDERED

SEX IS GOOD EXERCISE FOR YOUR HEART

Sex, as in 'making love', is mentally and physically exhausting. As it is a mixture of emotions. stresses and physical activity it can be 'overdone' as well as underdone. But it is good exercise. I mentioned that a short energetic activity such as weight-lifting can damage your health. and sporadic activities such as the 'Parent's Day Mile Run for Out-of-Shape Fathers'. are unwise and dangerous.

We can't expect to take any form of exercise – only once in a while – at full tilt! As in other forms of strenuous exercise there should be a 'warm-up' period before, and a gradual 'cooling down' period afterwards.

Sex can be strenuous and it is certainly good for you if you are fit. and even if you are not fit – although it raises your pulse rate. elevates your blood pressure. and puts a strain on muscle that you may not normally use – it shouldn't hurt you. But under certain circumstances it has been known to kill.

'The cardiac patient is no longer considered to be at high risk during sexual activity.'

78

'Average cardiac and metabolic expenditures during four sexual activities (coitus with husband on top; coitus with wife on top; noncoital stimulation of the husband by the wife; and self-stimulation by the husband) were measured in 10 healthy men and found to be the equivalent of light to moderate exercise.'

'The difference in cardiac and metabolic expenditures among sexual activities suggest that, generally, patients can be advised that partner stimulation or self-stimulation to orgasm may involve less effort than coital activities, with man-on-top coitus usually involving the most effort.'

'Archives of Internal Medicine', September 1984, Vol 144 No 9. 'Heart Rate, Rate-Pressure Product, and Oxygen Uptake During Four Sexual Activities', Bohlen, Held, Sanderson & Patterson

This study showed that almost 75 per cent did not resume any sexual activity after a heart attack and 80 per cent had no advice about sex from a doctor. He might have told them (if they had discussed the matter with him, as one always should) to gradually resume their sex life but to avoid the 'man-on-top position'. It seems that the heart rate and blood pressure increase most during husband-on-top coitus. Gradual return to sexual activities should produce mild to moderate exercise but excessive strain or sudden excitement are to be avoided, so the report stated. After reading about the 'laboratory conditions' under which the tests were conducted (the husband wore an oxygen mask and had electrocardiograph wires and blood pressure cuffs attached to various parts of his body – and he was obliged to signal the beginning and end of orgasm by pressing a hand-held button) I was surprised that his blood pressure rose at all.

We know that many middle-aged businessmen have heart attacks after a long and hard day of business stress, followed by too much drink and a heavy late meal, usually away from home and the normal routine. This combination is bad enough for your health, but when a strange female enters the scene the odds for heart attack increase. By 'strange' I mean different from one's normal sexual partner – a new, sexual experience with someone other than your wife or husband can kill you – and I don't mean by getting caught and shot. The combination of the excitement and physical effort needed to consummate the illicit relationship along with the overeating and the booze and the business stress, can be too much. Your system, like a computer, can go into 'overload'. More men die in their sleep as the doctor's report will verify (although they in fact die making love in a hotel room), than you might imagine. Rather than exercising your expense account, it might be better to make sure that your medical insurance is up-to-date and then get a good night's sleep when away on company business. To avoid the complications of this scenario, remember, fidelity is healthier when it comes to sex!

HOLIDAYS MAY BE BAD FOR YOUR HEALTH

Excess, as we know, can lead to increased risks. We tend to change our daily routine when we go on holiday. To reduce everyday stress, enjoy a change and relax is excellent. But increased eating and drinking and new and exhausting leisure activities while on holiday can lead to disaster. The statistics for holiday illness show that heart attacks and strokes are the serious illnesses suffered most when on holiday. Many cases occur in people who normally lead sedentary lives with little or no exercise: they usually drive rather than walk and spend much of their day in an office. Fourteen million Britons holiday abroad and 1,400 die abroad each year. Spain, France and Greece are the countries where deaths are most frequent, because they are the countries that the British visit most often.

The best policy is to get into decent physical shape well before going on holiday and remember the word *moderation* in eating, drinking *and* physical activity. Don't try to make up for lost time, especially with strenuous exercise. Too much volleyball will surely give you stiff muscles the next day – but prolonged, strenuous activity, especially a competitive one, can court a heart attack. Don't try to do it all in two weeks.

GOUT – MORE THAN JUST A PAIN IN THE BIG TOE

On the first night of a summer holiday in Corfu I indulged in the local wine – the next day I had a painful, red and swollen big toe joint – an attack of gout. Gout is one of those illnesses that has inspired a thousand jokes, mainly associated with port-drinking old colonels and the aristocracy. In fact it is a condition that is largely inherited and is caused by an excess of uric acid in the blood, or by the inability of the kidneys to clear away sufficient uric acid. This causes the formation of crystals (monosodium biurate) in the tissues of a joint, with swelling and pain resulting. It is mainly a male problem.

Although gout can immobilise you almost instantly it may not be diagnosed immediately because of its similarity to arthritis. The good thing about gout is that it can disappear as quickly as it came, as the elevation of uric acid may only be a temporary state and the condition will clear up when the high uric acid level recedes.

To continue my story, the doctor, who was called Dr Zorbas, to the delight of my family who thought the whole thing was a joke anyway (it usually is to everyone but the sufferer, and believe me it hurts like hell!) said that the culprit was probably the local white wine and I was to eat a special soup (which looked and tasted like dishwater) for two days and nothing else! He prescribed some pills and with these and the dishwater the swelling was gone in two days. And then I stepped on a wasp!

81

Gout is directly related to diet. The chemicals responsible to create a high uric acid condition are found in fish roes, liver, offal, meat extracts, sweetbreads, sardines, additives in wine (hence the port fixation) such as strong red wine, port and heavy beers.

Gout may appear as a sprain in the foot or ankle that won't heal. However, your doctor can easily reduce pain and inflammation by prescribing long-term pills to lower your uric acid level, if he finds that is a necessary treatment. Gout is easily controllable but sometimes tricky to detect.

Gout may be associated with the development of CHD because people with gout tend to suffer from high blood pressure and high triglycerides.

HOW TO SURVIVE STRESS

An 'instant response' system was created for our survival in a primitive existence. A million years ago when man was threatened it wasn't by the tax man or a traffic jam – it was more likely to have been a dinosaur or one of the Flintstones, grunting and swinging a stone axe. He was alerted, his blood filled with adrenaline, his heart pumped, and physical action or combat soon followed. It was a stressful situation and the physical release for this pent-up preparatory energy was immediate.

Our bodies still react in the same physiological fashion to a stressful situation today, but the threat is more likely to be emotional rather than physical and without the physical release, or even an emotional one, as it is more likely to be suppressed than expressed or released. The frustrations and tensions of our daily lives help to form our personalities, and our reactions to stress may add to our personal risk factors for CHD. I react to stress by eating – it makes me feel better – 'when under pressure, eat something bad for you' seems to have been my motto. Therefore, stress can lead to excess. More smoking, eating and drinking. You may be able to cope with stress on its own, but it is a catalyst for other risk factors that might cause or further the development of CHD.

Aside from being a catalyst to increase other risk factors, emotional stress will affect your body chemistry.

FACT:
Stress can increase the pulse rate dramatically and possibly cause it to rise to a dangerous level and raise the

blood pressure rapidly. It can also activate stress hormones to increase the level of fat in the blood, almost instantly. We know that stress depresses the immune system, which is the body's only defence against malignant cells.

In *The Western Way of Death*, Doctors Carruthers & Taggart told how tests were made on racing drivers – a profession motivated by stress – to see how blood fats and the heart were affected. Between the time the race started, to crossing the finishing line, the drivers' heart rates rose from a normal rate of 60-70 beats a minute to 200. Before the race the drivers' blood samples were clear – afterwards they were shown to be a whiteish colour with an increased fat content. The level of stress hormones, which tend to increase the heart rate had doubled before the race and were four times higher by the end. Even moderate increases in stress hormones can significantly raise the amount of fat in the blood.

Although racing driving is an extreme example of a 'stress profession', other stressful situations have also proven that heartbeats are greatly increased. A cross-section of people, including doctors, were tested immediately before public speaking engagements. Their heart beats rose to between 120 and 180 a minute. Television reporters were found to have pulse rates of 150. These levels are greater than those you might reach during moderate exercise, and possibly even during heavy exercise.

SUDDEN CARDIAC DEATH

Sudden cardiac death is the name given to most deaths from coronary heart disease. Men or women who seem to be well, and who don't have advanced coronary artery disease, suddenly experience irregular heartbeats which result in a chaotic pumping rhythm by the heart called ventricular fibrillation (page 38). This deprives the brain of blood and oxygen and in a few minutes death occurs – unless the heart can be made to stop beating so erratically. Of course some of these people have severely narrowed arteries, but it has been determined that many of the deaths are preventable. Death is usually caused by a temporary blockage of a coronary artery due to coronary artery spasm or platelet-clumping. Stress has been implicated as a cause of these unusual events.

FACT:
Platelets help blood to clot and if clotting occurs inside the arteries it can cause thrombosis – a reduction or stoppage of flow of blood to the heart.

Once again 'cholesterol the killer' is involved in this situation. High blood cholesterol may stimulate the blood platelets to develop a stickiness that causes them to clump together and form a clot (as will cigarette smoking). This process also releases the chemical thromboxane A_2. I realise that this is becoming a bit technical. but it's worth putting up with the chemical jargon for the moment. Thromboxane A_2 also causes coronary artery spasm. which means simply that the muscular wall of the artery constricts. like a leg muscle cramp. cutting off the flow of blood in the artery.

FACT:
Change in heart rate and arterial diameter are controlled by receptors on the heart and arteries. These are activated by adrenaline – a stress hormone. There are two types of receptors. Alpha and Beta. When Alpha receptors are stimulated. the arteries constrict. When Beta receptors are stimulated. the arteries dilate.

Now the plot thickens because noradrenaline (another

stress hormone) activates the Alpha receptor, thereby making the coronary arteries constrict. Also adrenaline and noradrenaline stimulate platelet clumping, and release thromboxane A_2 which, as we know, causes coronary artery spasm. And any of these chemicals can narrow the interior of the artery and obstruct the flow of blood to the heart.

Emotional stress can cause high levels of fatty acids including cholesterol in the blood, thereby increasing the secretion of noradrenaline and adrenaline into the bloodstream and increasing the possibility of arterial spasm.

If the spasm is severe enough it could stop the flow of blood even in an artery that doesn't have any fixed blockage. Platelet-clumping within the artery wall can create a blood clot, therefore many combinations are possible, triggered off by an emotional cause. A spasm can also cause an arterial wall, already hardened by a build-up of cholesterol, to crack and rupture, causing plaque haemorrhage resulting in a blood clot and obstruction.

'We can probably obtain as much information about a given patient's risk of dying by talking about what's going on in his life as by conducting an exhaustive examination with the latest in medical technology.

Dr Thomas B. Grayboys of Harvard Medical School in *The New England Journal of Medicine*, August 30, 1984

'The twentieth-century epidemic (CHD) seems due to the changes in the ways in which people eat and sleep, work and play, relate to one another, and react emotionally as well as to the socio-cultural circumstances under which they live. Similarly, the decline in CHD mortality in the United States, now more than 30 per cent less than the 1968 level, is attributed to changes in life-styles and behaviours. (Havlic and Feinlieb, 1979).

C. David Jenkins, Professor of Preventive Medicine and Community Health, University of Texas Medical Branch Hospitals, 1983 (from *Prevention of CHD* by Kaplan & Stamler)

Looking back on my mental state in 1967, I am certain that I was heading for a heart attack. Once you become aware, you can usually sense when your blood pressure is high and when the combination of situations in your life is not doing your health any good. The description of a Type A personality on page 60 could have been me. I was quick-tempered, aggressive, competitive, and the strain that I was under showed in my face, my body language and my behaviour towards all those around me. I wasn't too much fun to be with when I was irritable – and that was almost all the time.

Each one of us copes with stress differently. Sitting in traffic, or stuck behind a car going 25 miles an hour on a single lane road, when you are in a hurry, is a modern stressful situation. Along with the other changes in lifestyle that we must make, a different approach to stress and daily life is needed. But once again, fear will work wonders. I didn't change my personality overnight, but I tried to understand why I did certain things, and how my actions were irritating others, and hurting myself. Once you become aware that you are putting yourself at risk by your behaviour and the way you react to situations and people, you are self-destructive if you refuse to do something about it.

You might say, 'That's the way I am' but that's not strictly true. You may be exactly that truculent, hyper-active, perfectionist bastard because your blood pressure is too high and you push yourself constantly to the limit. Most of us can learn to control our excess emotions, learn to become aware of the signs that elevate our blood pressure and allow stress hormones to flow. What I did was leave Los Angeles to pursue a new life in Europe. Obviously this was the extreme. But others have either come to accept the circumstances or changed jobs, or revised their way of life to eliminate some of the stress-causing factors. Some have left their jobs and taken up their hobbies full time, obviously not something possible for the majority. It is difficult to make the break, to abandon what you do well and seek some other, perhaps less financially rewarding, role. But after all, you only live once and it might as well be for as long as possible.

If your problem is that you're unhappy with situations that are within your control, you must do something about them. Once again your doctor is the person to consult. But the simple prescription of a tranquillizer is not the complete answer. It may, however, be the temporary answer if the doctor feels it is necessary to relieve your stress through drugs. But the best way is for you yourself to isolate the problem and deal with it. I know this is easy for me to say, but it is vitally necessary. Once I was happy within myself and in an environment that suited me, I found it much easier to change my diet and my way of life. It was also easier because I left Los Angeles for southern Spain, where my downfall, hamburgers, hot dogs and ice-cream, were not up to my connoisseur addict standards! In certain countries you develop a healthier diet out of need rather than choice. Some of us are food junkies. An uncle who has a history of strokes (as did my mother) still takes his dog for a walk every evening – which is his excuse for going to his favourite ice-cream place and sneaking a chocolate milkshake. His arteries are already narrowed – he is poisoning himself, and he knows it. Yet the urge and need to have the ice-cream is greater than his need to survive. I understand his yearning but not his rationalisation.

Over a period of time I've worked out a diet that suits me. Now that I have controlled my food addictions, I eat all those things I like in moderation.

WE ALL HAVE ANXIETY ATTACKS!

Sometimes fears and emotions get the better of us – the fear can be an immediate and conscious one or will brew for weeks or months in the subconscious. We all recognise the feeling – I call it the 'mental sweats' – that clammy sensation at 3 A.M. when you can't sleep, or when you're stuck in a traffic jam or are facing an important meeting. Everyone reacts to periods of stress – sometimes with panic.

It can be very difficult to cope. We must learn how to do it. Lifestyle changes will help. Certain foods cause forms of stress. Caffeine (in coffee, tea and soft drinks) is a stress stimulant. Moderation in your consumption of caffeine may ease a certain degree of stress in your diet and lifestyle. I now drink decaffeinated coffee as I found that more than three or four cups of coffee a day made me feel tense and nervous and caused an irritated stomach.

In spite of ourselves the mind plays games and controls the body. A few months after I had my angiogram I visited my wife's family in Yorkshire. During dinner I suddenly felt my pulse racing. I knew it was very fast and, for some reason, panicked sending my pulse even higher. The local hospital admitted me fearing a heart attack. In fact what I had had was an 'anxiety attack' – for some reason fear took over and helped to raise my pulse rate and blood pressure.

Research by industrial as well as medical organisations is trying to define the type of person who is most at risk from stress-related coronary heart problems. It is difficult to define this person, but the researchers are getting closer.

Scientist Redford Williams of Duke University Medical Centre says 'we suggest that cynicism captures the toxic element in the Type A personality.'

Type A personality includes many beneficial traits but mistrustful people produce more 'fight or flight' hormones than do less cynical folk. These hormones may accelerate plaque build-up on artery walls.

89

I contrasted earlier the different Type A and Type B personalities and I'm sure that most people seem to fit into either one category or another. Some of the traits of a Type A personality are necessary for success and survival in the business world. Recent studies have shown that there are people who move between these two groups, adapting to situations by combining the traits of each into their personality. 'Hard work won't kill you, but the worrying will' is something I remember from childhood as part of a work ethic. A Type B approach to dealing with the work pressure is the form to achieve. Long hours of high level performance combined with a creative, constructive atmosphere and environment is good. The destructive elements of impatience, excessive competitive drive, ambitiousness and an over zealous desire to achieve a constant atmosphere of urgency, the tendency to take on multiple commitments, an undue concern for meeting deadlines, an inability to relax without feeling guilty, the drive to accomplish tasks quickly – these are all *bad* reactions to stress.

AT WORK

Stress-related illnesses cost America £53 billion a year and Britain £7½ billion a year. Up to ten times more workdays are lost to industry through stress than strikes (*The Economist*, July 7, 1984). Coronary heart disease does the most damage, accounting for about half the cost of stress-related illness. Stress does not acknowledge rank or sex – bosses, managers, workers all risk suffering a mental breakdown or alcoholism, drug dependence, ulcers, suicides.

The job itself with its workplace or environment together with the boss-worker relationship may be strong determinants of CHD. The workers who will be at risk feel they don't have the boss on their side and turn to their family for support, thus alienating themselves from the work environment further. Workers who have a sense of commitment and are enjoying a challenge at their jobs will feel that they are exercising control over their lives. There are also many people with jobs which make considerable demands upon them but give them no say in decision-making. The resultant frustration may lead to a heart attack.

The American Management Association looked at the problem within the office environment and found that Type As were inclined to be 'workaholic' and tended to speed up themselves as well as their co-workers, in times of stress. Type Bs, though ambitious and successful in their jobs, reacted to stress by changing their normal work routine to provide periods of rest and relaxation throughout the day and actually achieved more from themselves and from their fellow workers. These people used *stress management* strategies effectively. Stress Management is one of those American-sounding phrases that smacks of jargon, but it is good shorthand to explain what I mean. These Type B persons were able to delegate some of the responsibility rather than trying to do it all themselves. They also analysed their situation and what would cause them stress and then decided what had priority and what not to worry about. They were organised and established daily goals and objectives.

'Even brief rises of blood pressure, if they occur many thousands of times, may tend to damage vulnerable portions of the internal surface of blood vessel walls. Both laboratory and clinical studies have shown that acute emotional stresses can provoke cardiac arryhthmias and sudden death.'

C. David Jenkins PhD
Prevention of CHD, by Kaplan and Stamler, W. P. Saunders Co., London, 1983.

A sensible approach to a busy schedule is to be more easy-going, even though efficiency and high levels of achievement are the goals. Enjoy your work. Your work style should show a lack of a sense of urgency, without the need to display achievement and with no hostility shown to the people around you. Enjoy your leisure. Sports or hobbies should be relaxing without undue emphasis on competition. The ability to relax without guilt, and work under pressure and deadlines without agitation or irritability is your aim. You're the one at risk! Of course some of you will say 'that's impossible!' It is difficult, but it's not impossible.

Meyer Friedman, one of the doctors who labelled the Type A personality in his book (M. Friedman, R. H. Rosenman, *Type A behaviour and your heart*. Alfred A. Knopf, New York, 1974), has recently reported that hard-driving behaviour is sometimes reversible – those of us who slow down and remove some of the self-inflicted pressure, significantly lower our risk of suffering heart attacks. He suggests that drugs to block the hormones causing these stress-related coronary heart problems should be prescribed rather than trying to modify behaviour. My feeling is that both should be done. We must all try to change any behaviour pattern that might damage our health, whether we do it by meditation, sheer willpower, or, if we need help in the beginning, a prescribed drug, after consultation with a doctor. 'Behavioural modification' (another piece of jargon) is a self-help approach within our control.

Changing a Type A personality isn't very easy because in our society this behaviour is usually rewarded with a better job, more money and applause. Trying to change may make a person prone to more anxiety, frustration and anger. An atmosphere of restraint, less aggression and tension is not what a Type A would voluntarily submit himself to – even for his personal good.

A recent US study (Beta-Blocker Heart Attack Trial, as

reported in *New England Journal of Medicine*, August, 30, 1984) of 2,320 men showed that after three years of treatment the risk of death was related to high levels of life stress and to relatively high levels of social isolation.

LONELINESS IS BAD FOR YOU

A close-knit social structure that gives emotional and social support is thought to lower the incidence of CHD. The more people are connected by having an understanding marriage partner and/or close contact with friends and relatives outside their work environment, the better chance they have of a healthy and longer life. The family and social circle seem to offer protection. I can hear some of you saying, 'If you only knew my family!'

Obviously bad marriages and family problems don't fall into this category. Unemployed people, students and people who are under extreme pressure all have been found to have increased cholesterol levels as have accountants at the end of the tax year. In a test of these groups of people their cholesterol levels went up by 20 per cent during these stressful periods, even though they had not altered their diet.

A study by the Health Insurance Plan of Greater New York found that lonely men in low level jobs or with other stresses in their lives are four times more likely to die after a heart attack than men with few emotional and family burdens. They found a higher level of stress and social isolation among less-educated heart attack victims. This seems to shatter the myth that the archetypal heart attack victim is the high-living, ambitious, over-achieving executive.

In *The Lancet*, March 17, 1984, A. H. Crisp, M. Queenan & M. S. De Souza state that people destined for a heart attack tend to be more obsessional and are greater worriers than others. In the year before the attack they displayed high levels of sadness, anxiety-related symptoms, loss of libido, fatigue unrelated to angina and a fear of an incurable illness. This 'worrying' attitude may influence tobacco smoking, eating, general activity, and perhaps, immune and neuroendocrine systems as part of their direct and indirect impact on the cardiovascular system. It is well-known that people who have recently suffered an emotional disaster such as a death in the family, a divorce, or the loss of a job, have a higher incidence of heart attacks.

A situation that we are powerless to change or affect is inherently stressful. (If we know that it is caused by *our* actions and reactions then we can do something about it – we can try to react in healthier ways.) The 'signs of stress' are there – palpitation, irritability, tiredness and drinking. Unfortunately there is a link between 'excellence' and early death from heart disease. The 'excellent' managers are highly competitive, aggressive, impatient, restless, bad at delegating and lack outside interests – many of the qualities associated with business success. (*The Economist*, July 7, 1984.)

'Helplessness and a sense of ultimate defeat do render some individuals vulnerable to early illness. Alternatively, at least some elements of such experiential states may, in this instance, reflect otherwise symptomless developing myocardial damage.'

A. H. Crisp, M. Queenan & M. S. De Souza, *The Lancet*, March 17, 1984.)

Unbearable frustration or temporary inability to cope may be dealt with through sleep, relaxation exercise, diet and 'talking it out'. Meyer Friedman has advised that we: stop doing more than one thing at a time; learn to listen without interrupting; escape into books that demand concentration; learn to eat slowly and taste the food; have a private retreat in the home; plan some idleness every day; avoid contact with people who stimulate harmful reactions; try to organise vacations and trips to avoid time pressures. Going on holiday might be more stressful than going to work.

Just as you looked in the mirror earlier for signs of a person at risk, it is now necessary to analyse how you react to stress. As I explained earlier I used to react very badly. Now, *before* I react I force myself to analyse the situation and think about how to approach it. And then I panic! But often I will channel the stress and the anticipated fears and energy into achieving the task or goal more efficiently – even if this is a slower, more analytical process. Formerly I always jumped headlong into a situation, trying to resolve it with speed and intense energy – creating a stressful environment for myself and for those around me.

If stress has already resulted for you in high blood pressure or an elevated blood cholesterol level your doctor will help, but now that you are aware of this stress in your life you must learn to deal with it. Many books and magazine articles have been written on the subject and there are different answers for different people. I know that exercise, a change in diet and physical fitness and weight control have helped me. Stress management techniques such as meditation, breathing exercise and deep relaxation yoga exercises have been successful in treating hypertension and even used to lower cholesterol levels – independent of dietary changes. Hobbies such as gardening, needlepoint and reading can slow you down and relax you. Visit your local sports centre and take up a new sport, learn how to swim, or improve your style and stamina. Swimming may be the best exercise of all. But remember *before* you do anything – always discuss it with your doctor first!

The main objective is a new awareness within yourself that will lead to better health and the control over the parts of your life that are within your control.

DANGER SIGNALS – HOW TO RECOGNISE IF YOU ARE AT RISK FROM STRESS

There are certain signs that show stress as having an effect on your well-being. These signals may become apparent six months, a year, or more before a heart attack strikes. You may experience weariness or mental exhaustion. This can be caused by events at home or at work that upset you. Normal daily existence can become a major struggle and things that you didn't even think about before take increased effort and energy to accomplish.

Fatigue or abnormal physical tiredness is another danger signal. An active person puts demands upon the heart and body to keep the energy level high and constant. Once the heart doesn't fill these physical demands you may lose your physical stamina and tiredness, rather than pain is felt. Depression will also cause a feeling of tiredness.

Certain behavioural patterns may accelerate deteriorating health such as a constant search for happiness and personal satisfaction in goal achievement. All people with high standards and ambition set goals including material ones, but a feeling of waiting for 'the real thing' to happen is bad. It interferes with the enjoyment of what is happening now, and it is far more important for your well being for you to begin to enjoy the means as well as deriving pleasure from the ends. Pleasure in certain material goals may be short-lived and disappointing.

Rushing and worrying and angry emotions can raise the blood pressure. This can result in an over-aroused and exhausted way of life that will cause unhealthy changes in your blood. An addiction to work and constant tension can be bad if it causes a feeling of mental tiredness.

In 1967 T. H. Holmes and R. H. Rahe established that certain events which change the normal pattern of life are stressful. They gave points to show the degree to which each event disturbed a person.

100	death of a spouse
73	divorce
60–69	personal injury or illness
50	marriage
40–49	loss of a job, marital reconciliation, retirement, change in health or a family member, pregnancy
30–39	sex difficulties, new family member, business readjustment, change of financial condition, death of a close friend, change to a different line of work, change in number of arguments with spouse, large mortgage.
20–29	foreclosure of mortgage or loan, change in responsibilities at work, son or daughter leaving home, trouble with in-laws, outstanding personal achievement, wife begins or stops work, change in living conditions, revision of personal habits, trouble with boss, change in work, house or conditions, change in residence.
10–19	Changes in recreation, church, or school activities, small mortgage, minor violation of law, change in eating/sleeping habits, number of family get-togethers, vacation, Christmas.

The danger level will vary for each individual, but to generalise the scoring, a score of 60 points for half a year and a score of more than 150 for one year is a sign of an unhealthy change in your life. People who are approaching a coronary breakdown have scores of 400 to 600 for two or three years. This type of score will reflect a life struggle that is exhausting and physically damaging.

The process of mental and physical decline through stress becomes a downward spiral. When you are used to functioning in a certain way at a very active level, any weakness will force you to try to use more strength and energy than you have – just to continue your normal pace of life. If you fall behind you try harder to make up for lost time and begin steadily to slide back and work even harder. The result is frustration and exhaustion. Your health will then suffer. At this point it is important to recognize what is going on (most of us don't, as we are too involved and possibly afraid of admitting what is beginning to happen) and to plan to reorganise your life to meet this new change and to adjust to it.

Analyse what is getting on top of you. What is causing you to lose your grip on events? What is the source of the stress and worry?

Reduce the overload on your life. Stop for a moment and remove the pressure and look at the situation objectively.

You may be headed for a mental or physical breakdown unless you withdraw, try to relax, get your strength back and then renew the fight. Continuing at reduced strength will result in failure and more guilt. Once you are healthy again you stand a better chance of success.

Evaluate your assets and liabilities, including your friends and relationships within your family, and avoid self-deception. It may be the time to face a few emotional truths.

Try to anticipate future relationships and events that might increase the strain and cause you more pressure, tension and frustration. It may be time for a few changes.

Admit that failure may be a possibility and adjust your life to creating an environment and situations where you can win.

If you are having trouble sleeping, please see your doctor. Sleep is a vital part of any programme to regain your energy and vitality. One of the first signs that the stress and problems are getting to you physically is difficulty with sleep. So many of us suffer from this problem without realising its significance. In anxiety states and cases of depression there is a difficulty in falling asleep.

It is usually caused by an unresolved emotional problem. If there were problems during the day at work or emotions that couldn't be expressed, these will cause unresolved anxiety or anger. Emotional problems at home will complicate and increase the problem. At bedtime these emotions may force you to stay awake as they surge through your mind.

Regular early morning waking

Over the last few years I have noticed that during periods of intense work pressure and stress, I have no trouble falling asleep but at between three and four in the morning I wake up, usually totally alert. Unfortunately the first thoughts that I have are about those problems that were difficult to resolve before going to sleep. I've since found out that sometimes this can be a symptom of depressive illness and is a warning that may precede serious illness.

People who experience this have no difficulty sleeping earlier in the evening, in fact they might fall into a deep sleep on the sofa in front of the TV. Their mood and attitude upon waking in the early hours is usually gloomy, depressed and sometimes with a dread of facing the next day's events and problems. They may fall back to sleep but when they awake later their personality is different from that after normal relaxed sleep. With increasing unresolved worries their attitude lacks a normal aggression or optimism. There is a tendency towards a concern with trivia and minor problems which may result in impaired judgement. There is a tendency to look at the negative side of things, dwelling on failure – both past and projected – a feeling of hopelessness, or forthcoming disaster, and a lack of self-esteem or worthiness. If you've ever experienced early morning waking for any length of time you'll know how emotionally draining it can be – not to mention how physically tired you soon become.

However, with treatment these depressive illnesses can be cured and once the person recovers there is usually no permanent psychological damage or even a repeat of the problem.

DANGER SIGNALS

— Type A personality – (impatient, fierce competitive drive, chronic sense of urgency, taking on more tasks than are possible to do in an orderly way)
— cynical attitude towards life
— obsessional personality
— tendency to be a worrier, even when there is no need
— loss of libido
— unexplained fatigue and weariness
— fear of incurable illness
— chronic sadness, depression, frequent anxiety attacks
— social isolation from family or friends
— satisfaction only with goals achieved – refusal to enjoy the means and what good is happening *now*
— a constant waiting for life to begin rather than short term goals and satisfaction
— inability to take on responsibilities or make decisions, where you were able to before
— angry emotions that become part of the normal personality, first and immediate reaction is to become aggressive and quick-tempered
— feeling of helplessness and ultimate defeat
— sleeplessness – early morning waking

EVENTS IN YOUR LIFE THAT INCREASE RISK OF CHD

— a death in the immediate family
— divorce or separation
— loss or change of job – possibility of redundancy
— emotional difficulty at home – or at work
— moving house and job to another country, or area
— major financial problems
— illness

PREVENTIVE MEDICINE

'Doctors should break free from a narrow professionalism and do more for health education. The medical profession has to re-examine its responsibilities to prevention.'

Prof M. F. Oliver, *British Medical Journal*, February 11, 1984

There are many of us walking around who, as Prof Geoffrey Rose put it, are 'almost patients'. The care of the person at risk who has no symptoms is *preventive medicine*.

We are all familiar with the fact that preventive medicine saves lives. Inoculations protect us against polio, smallpox, diphtheria, tetanus and other infectious diseases.

We brush our teeth to prevent plaque and cavities; we wear protective clothing for dangerous work and sports. Preventive actions such as wearing seat-belts can save us from injury, disabilities and death through accident.

Preventive medicine tries to do something about illness *before* it happens.

Therapeutic medicine treats sickness and disease *after* it happens, which includes pills to reduce high blood pressure, and operations, such as heart transplants.

Some preventive medicine is guaranteed by law, (e.g. quarantine for animals entering the UK to prevent the spread of rabies).

Much is *recommended* and good sense tells us to comply with the information we are given. Of course some free spirits choose to ride horses and motor bikes without protective helmets, and the deaths and serious injuries from these actions prove this to be a dangerous and foolish act. But the fact remains that medical experts can only tell us what is good for our health and safety – they cannot force us to comply. Each of us weighs the possibility of accidents happening to us against the inconvenience it will cause us to comply with the safety regulations.

Deaths from car accidents fell sharply after people were made by law to wear seat belts.

We are told smoking cigarettes is bad and so are drugs, but lung cancer from smoking and drug addiction are still major international social problems.

GOVERNMENT POLICY TOWARDS THE NATIONAL DIET

For more than ten years the British Government has known exactly what should be done to start to decrease the mortality rate from coronary heart disease in the UK (via the DHSS 'Diet and Coronary Heart Disease', Report of the Advisory Panel of the Committee on Medical Aspects of Food Policy (Nutrition) on Diet in Relation to Cardio-vascular and Cerebrovascular Disease, 1974).

Yet the government did nothing to create a National Dietary Policy that had become priority in the United States, Canada, Australia, Finland and throughout the rest of Europe. The World Health Organization's Expert Committee recommended a policy 'Prevention of Coronary Heart Disease', under its British chairman Prof Geoffrey Rose in 1982.

In 1984 the National Advisory Committee on Nutrition Education (NACNE) Report was published but not given the government backing it merited. The NACNE Report recommended a reduction in fat intake, the avoidance of obesity and the moderation of salt and sugar intake as well as an increase in dietary fibre. Although the NACNE

Report was supported by the Royal College of Physicians, the British Cardiac Society and the World Health Organization, as well as most major government and medical bodies throughout the world, the Report was suppressed for two years by the government for being too radical, but was finally published in 1984. The aims of the committee were 'compromised' and the recommendations it finally made were far below those adopted in most other countries – those standards that have inspired and motivated a change in national diets and have saved lives.

In 1984, the DHSS Committee on Medical Aspect of Food Policy (COMA) gave its 'Report of the Panel on Diet in Relation to Cardiovascular Disease', just ten years after the 1974 report. In the *British Medical Journal*, September 1, 1984, A. Stewart Truswell, Professor of Human Nutrition at the University of Sydney, said:

'Mortality from coronary heart disease has been static in Britain since 1974, when the Department of Health published its first report on diet and coronary disease . . . Britain has not shared in the declining mortality from coronary heart disease which started in the United States and is now being experienced in Australia, Belgium, Canada, Finland, New Zealand, Norway, and some other Western countries. Consequently Scotland, Northern Ireland, and England with Wales have moved up in the world league table of coronary deaths to second, third, and fifth positions respectively for men, and first, second and ninth positions for women. No reduction of average fat consumption has taken place in this country; from 1974 to 1982 it crept up from 40 per cent to 41 per cent of food energy, and plasma cholesterol concentrations may still be rising . . . here is a very sensible report. It should be the basis for concerted national effort . . . Health education in Britain has been ineffective so far in reducing coronary heart disease!'

The COMA Panel was made up of some of the most respected members of the British, and indeed international, medical establishment, which included Prof W. P. T. James (NACNE); Prof G. A. Rose (World Health Organization); Prof M. F. Oliver (Univ of Edinburgh); and the Chairman Prof P. J. Randle (Univ of Oxford).

The Report stated that 'in England and Wales death from coronary heart disease causes the annual loss of 250,000 years of "working life", with nearly 30,000 deaths in men under the age of 65.' It went on to make recommendations to the general public, doctors, producers and manufacturers of food and drink, and to Government, 'regarding nutrition with the object of decreasing the incidence of cardiovascular diseases in general and of coronary heart disease in particular'. The Report is clear both in its language and its direction.

Some of the statements it made are:

— Recommendations regarding nutrition should afford 'improvement in life expectancy overall, and in the quality of life for the population as a whole'. This includes all of us who are high risks for CHD and others who are not.
— It confirms, 'it is possible to identify, by clinical and laboratory investigation, individuals who have an increased risk of coronary heart disease. We believe it is important to identify such individuals, and to give consideration to ways and means of facilitating their identification, so that special advice may be given to them'.
— 'There is sufficient consistency in the evidence to make it more likely than not that the incidence of coronary heart disease will be reduced, or its age of onset delayed, by decreasing dietary intake of saturated fatty acids and total fat.'

104

— 'The report of the Expert Committee of the World Health Organization has recommended that the dietary energy derived from saturated fatty acids should be limited to ten per cent and that from fat to 30 per cent of food energy. Our recommendations of 35 per cent (total fat) and of 15 per cent (saturated plus trans fatty acids) are designed to take account of practical considerations in the United Kingdom.'

— 'The Panel sees advantages in compensating for a reduced fat intake with increased fibre-rich carbohydrates (e.g. bread, cereals, fruit, vegetables,) provided that this can be achieved without increasing total intake of common salt or simple sugars.

— 'We recommend that people should not smoke cigarettes.

— 'Those responsible for health education should inform the general public of the recommendations and how to implement them . . . compliance depends critically upon the level and quality of counselling given to participants.'

— 'Means should be found to educate the general population of the United Kingdom in habits of eating and physical activity that will minimize the risk of cardio-vascular disease and obesity. The process of education should be started in schools.'

— 'There has been a progressive increase in the average weight for height of adults in Britain over the last 40 years and by 1981 over 40 per cent of middle-aged men and women were overweight. The environmental factors accounting for this weight increase are many including a decline in physical activity and change in dietary patterns.'

— 'The major sources of fatty acids are milk and cream (approx $\frac{1}{5}$), meat and meat products (approx $\frac{1}{4}$), butter, margarines and cheese (approx $\frac{1}{3}$) and cooking fats and oils (approx $1/10$), ... About 40 per cent of the decreases in saturated fatty acids and fat recommended nationally could be achieved by avoiding cream, replacing whole milk with semi-skimmed milk and switching to the lower fat cheeses.'

The entire Report was carefully worded to reflect a policy that its many members could endorse, and as always, there were conflicting opinions which were expressed in a statement in the Preface:

'The Panel, in its consideration of the complex relationship between diet and cardiovascular disease, has acknowledged that the evidence falls short of proof. Nevertheless, in the opinion of the members, it is sufficiently consistent that, if changes in the diet occur in the directions recommended, benefits to health are likely.'

I agree with their recommendations but feel that a more aggressive attitude is needed to catch up with the progress that is being made in other parts of the world. Caution is important but 'action' is the priority – and fast!

'Coronary Heart Disease Prevention – Plans for Action' was a report based on a workshop conference held at Canterbury in September 1983, with a very impressive list of sponsors and co-sponsors, which included the Health Education Council, the Department of Health and Social Security, the British Cardiac Society, the Coronary Prevention Group as well as the British Medical Association and many Royal Colleges and medical associations. The Canterbury Report clearly expressed 'The Need for Action'. It stressed that, 'The contribution of medical or surgical therapy is limited, both by the scale and by the nature of

106

the problem. Prevention is essential. Prevention implies the correction of causes.' It states that, 'coronary heart disease has become a mass disease because of unhealthy characteristics of "average" life-style. This is a difficult concept, because it runs counter to the natural assumption that what most people do is alright. It points to a need for change in some widely accepted norms.'

The objectives of the conference were:

— To identify practical and efficient strategies for implementing in the United Kingdom the main recommendations of the 1982 WHO Expert Committee Report on the 'Prevention of Coronary Heart Disease'

— To examine the consequent implications for relevant areas of public policy.

The ultimate aim was for 'effective and speedy action to prevent coronary heart disease'.

The Report went on to say:

— 'The main aim with regard to preventing coronary heart disease should be reduction of its risk.

— The scientific basis for a policy on heart disease prevention has been reviewed in many authoritative reports, including the Joint Report by the Royal College of Physicians and the British Cardiac Society (1976). Despite a remarkable agreement in their main recommendations, little has been done to implement them.

— The UK, as yet, has no national strategy for the promotion of health or the prevention of disease. There is an urgent need for the British Government through the Department of Health to formulate national policies and programmes for health promotion and disease prevention.'

The Canterbury Report goes on to explain in detail how there can be action within the food and agricultural industries, the Department of Health, through the National Health Service. Primary Health Care, Health Education and action through the mass media.

There are masses of government-sponsored reports and thousands of man hours spent by some of the best scientific and medical people in the UK (who are world experts in their fields) and still there is no agreed national policy for nutrition and health education.

Atherosclerosis is the major cause of social disability in the United States, and scored top in the resulting limitation of activity of sufferers, top in the number of hospital days spent in bed and top in terms of the number of physician visit days with over 30 million in 1980. Heart and blood vessel diseases are estimated to cost the United States government some 50,000 million dollars each year in lost wages, lost productivity and expenses for medical care (R. I. Levy). The costs in the UK are high, not only in money spent by the NHS to treat CHD and heart attacks, and the increase in expensive surgery such as bypasses, but also to the families who are hit by loved ones suffering disabling heart attacks – at an increasingly earlier age.

We know the risk factors. Each of us is different: some are high risk, some low; others can eat, drink and do what they like and they may never develop a heart problem. Some risk factors may be inherited but environmental and other factors are totally within our control.

WHAT CAN BE DONE

All of us need to become more aware of the preventive approach to CHD – and this includes G.P.s, cardiologists and other consultants. Therapeutic medicine ranging from the use of drugs to reduce anxiety and stress, to lower cholesterol levels, lower blood pressure, and reduce blood clotting, to prevent coronary artery spasm, to surgical means of correcting the existing problems such as coronary bypass surgery and ileal bypass surgery (correcting cholesterol overproduction in the intestine) are all valid and important procedures that the medical profession follows to beat heart disease. But it is necessary that changes to reduce environmental and behavioural coronary risk factors should be prescribed as well. Coronary bypass surgery may provide an alternative route for the blood circulation, avoiding the arteries clogged with atheroma, but the surgery won't stop whatever caused the fatty build-up within the artery in the first instance.

Preventive measures are needed not only *before* a person has the first attack, but *after* as well. We (both doctors and patients) must do everything we can to slow up the progression of CHD, and that includes changes in diet and reduction of other risk factors. The new bypass grafts must be prevented from clogging up, just as the original coronary arteries did, or else in a number of years the patient will be back to square one. The cause of the problem must be addressed, as well as trying to treat the manifestations of the disease or illness. The medical profession remains divided regarding the extent to which CHD incidence and mortality could be reduced by dietary changes. *The Lancet* presents two views to answer the question, 'How much benefit?'

'One view is exemplified by the report of a WHO Expert Committee, chaired by Prof Geoffrey Rose. This points out that most cases of IHD occur among the larger number in whom risk factors, including cholesterol, are only moderately raised, and not among the small numbers with high values, "Only a mass (population) approach can help this larger group." The implications are that a downward shift in the entire distribution of a risk factor such as cholesterol is necessary. But if this shift could be achieved, the reduction in incidence and mortality would probably be considerable. The other view has lately been summarized by Prof Michael Oliver . . . He suggests abandoning the mass control of coronary risk factors on several grounds, and advocates a strategy of identifying and concentrating on those at particularly high risk, even though they are in the minority.'

The Lancet, Aug 6, 1983. 'Diet and Ischaemic Heart Disease – agreement or not?'

There are two contrasting theories on tackling this problem. One, favoured by the epidemiologists (people who study problems from a social point of view, how it affects geographical areas, classes, men, women, etc.), is to put into operation a 'mass intervention' programme. This would attempt to reduce as many of the risk factors in as many people as possible, and to spread information and treatment to everyone to reduce heart disease throughout the population. The best way to accomplish this is to use the media to educate the public about diet and exercise as well as about the risk factors that contribute to the progression of CHD. This awareness in the general public should shift the cholesterol levels downwards – provided people do what is strongly recommended for their general health. This method has worked in the United States and other countries.

The second method favoured by the specialists who have a more clinical approach, is 'high risk intervention' which means that all those families and individuals with the highest risk should be located for immediate treatment. This treatment would include diet, exercise and whatever programme of care that doctors would decide is necessary.

I agree with both approaches – both should be simultaneous priorities. I happen to be among the minority with a genetic, high risk problem which thankfully was discovered in time. Everything should be done to find other people like myself. both through the G.P.s locating us from their list of patients and through the public's own efforts. Each person should assess their own risk factors to find out if they do have FH or any other high risk condition and should present their case to their doctor. I realise that Americans are rather forward and brash and seemingly uninhibited at times, but it stems from the belief that most things are possible and are within our own control. We get carried away by this 'American Dream' complex occasionally, but it can sometimes be useful.

The time this attitude comes in handy is when your doctor tells you that nothing is wrong with you and yet you have a pain that hurts like hell – that's the time to make 'your stand'. If you have a history of heart attacks or stroke in immediate relatives younger than 55. and if you have some of the risk factors explained in Chapter 2 then you should have your blood pressure and blood cholesterol checked immediately. But the average British male (and female as well) feels that if he gives in to illness or admits he's sick then he's doing something wrong. CHD progresses silently most of the time and then strikes suddenly and fiercely – it's the cobra of the disease kingdom.

In most cases high risk patients can be treated and the imbalance restored to normal. But time is not on the side of people like me – it's a race against the sand in the hourglass – the sooner it's detected. the better off you will be. Finding out that you have CHD can be the *best*, not the *worst* day of your life. It will be the first day of your road to recovery, your health is back in your hands. and in your doctor's, not in the hands of fate and ignorance. It's far worse not to be doing anything about it. especially if, like myself. you can pass your illness on to your children: the odds are fifty/fifty. But. when discovered. the road to recovery has

111

started; CHD can be controlled and treated – and reversed!

The other approach to the general public, through telling all of us the facts about CHD, even if we don't have it, is a very important education. Each of us knows someone who has had or has died from a heart attack, and unfortunately some of these were very young people. Knowing about first aid, diet and exercise won't hurt, it can only help, even if you don't have CHD. Understanding nutrition and how to keep healthy is something that will improve your appearance, help you to feel better and fitter, help you to lose weight gradually and sensibly if you need, or want to, and allow you to develop healthier eating patterns. You all have the right to know the facts! Now that a scientific link between high cholesterol and heart disease is proven, a public programme of nutritional education should be a national priority. Food manufacturers should label all products that are high or low in saturated fats and cholesterol, as well as their calorie content. They should let us know what we are eating, other than just the generic brand or name, so we can make an intelligent choice with our health in mind if we wish. Some may choose to keep eating the way they have always done, even if it's eating fats and sugar and calories galore – it's their choice and also their right. But give us the facts! State the contents on the packets where we can see them *and* in language we all can understand.

In 1982, the July 3 issue of *The Lancet*, explained how it should work:

'The chain of events ought to be: scientific research leads to health education and Government advice; educated consumers then demand healthier foods; and the food suppliers respond, drawing on the science to back up marketing. Because the first link is not yet well forged (opponents of the fat/heart disease connection are still vocal), succeeding ones are inevitably weaker.'

112

Sir Jeremy Moore, the Director General of the Food and Drink Federation has stated, 'It is the industry's responsibility to provide a wide range of safe and wholesome foods for the consumer to choose from'. He noted that the COMA report (see p. 103) did not mean that there was a need for everyone to change his or her diet. I agree with him. Some of us are already health conscious and others have no medical or health reason to alter their present diet, or indeed, their way of life. My aim is to give you as much information as I can about your health, and to encourage you to speak to your doctor if you feel that you, or a member of your family is at risk. But if your blood cholesterol levels are normal and you are not dangerously overweight and you don't feel a personal need to refrain from eating any of the foods that are not good for people at risk, then as Sir Jeremy Moore has said, there is no reason for you to stop eating cream, butter, sausages, etc. But if you are one of the many of us at risk, you should want to alter these things.

Prof M. F. Oliver is very sympathetic to any measures which will reduce the incidence of coronary heart disease in those particularly at risk such as individuals with FH, and suggests:

'It should be easy to screen the families of patients with CHD although this is rarely done. The identification of families in which there is an excessive aggregation of vascular diseases (coronaries, strokes, and peripheral diseases) has received too little attention. I am continually astonished that the children and younger siblings of men and women who have developed CHD under the age of 50 are not screened systematically for the presence of risk factors.'

Current Medical Literature, *Cardiovascular Medicine*, 1984; 3(1): 4–9

The European Society of Cardiology and The Royal Society of Medicine.

' Looking after your body – eating healthy foods and exercising, giving up smoking and drinking a reasonable amount is a form of preventive medicine. We know that excess is not good for our health, and that moderation is the better policy.

EXERCISE

We all know that exercise is good for you and is recommended by every study as part of a fitness programme. The problem with exercise is that it takes up time and it is boring. No matter what books tell you, you can't keep your heart and body fit on five minutes a day. Exercise, in order to be effective, must be: *Regular* (three or four times a week); *Intense* (raise pulse rate for 20 to 30 minutes at a session); and *Progressive* (as you get stronger the exercise gets harder).

But the cure can be worse than the disease. As in diet, moderation is the operative word in exercise. Too much can be dangerous. Aerobic exercise gets the heart pumping, which is obviously beneficial, *but* overdoing it can hurt your heart and injure muscles. The first rule of a new exercise programme is *don't overdo it*. You must be basically fit before you push your body to new limits. Bring yourself up to a basic standard before you start training. This basic standard is different in all of us.

Once again, a visit to your doctor is always important if you have a heart condition or any other physical reason for limiting the amount or type of exercise you will do. Unlike a new hobby, exercise is an activity that you should not plunge into. Introduce your body gradually to a new regime. The fact that you played rugby ten years ago doesn't mean that you can jog a mile or more now. Moderation is required.

Whenever I see men in their forties and fifties puffing at school sports days, or village fetes, I fear for them. Any sudden strenuous exercise can hurt – you must build up to it. Don't accept challenges in running or sit-ups or push-ups to prove you're as fit as you used to be. Strenuous sports such as jogging or squash should not be undertaken once a week – play more often, or not at all. Why not swim instead, a few laps to start, slowly – then build it up. Avoid all the 'muscle burn' that the aerobic and jogging fanatics praise – it can cause a heart muscle 'burn-out'. Exercise cures – but too much, too soon, may kill.

Aerobics when not properly supervised or adapted to each person's state of health, fitness and physique can lead to back, joint and muscle injury. Intense aerobics can overtax the heart.

Every form of exercise if overdone can cause damage! Lifting weights can squeeze blood out of muscles instead of increasing blood flow to muscles; jogging can put too much strain on heart, back, spine and limbs and squash can cause severe strain on muscle tissue of the heart and can lead to abnormalities in the rhythmic pattern of heart beat.

Exercise burns up fat to produce energy. It also strengthens the muscles and increases the flow of blood and oxygen to all parts of your body, including heart, lungs and brain, thereby making the process more efficient. Your heart learns to work more effectively through proper exercise, as it pumps better and with more strength and less effort. Therefore your resting pulse rate, which determines how hard your heart is beating, gradually lowers. Men whose resting heart rates are above 90 die from coronary heart disease at a rate two and a half times greater than those with resting heart rates under 70. Exercise is one step in the process that will prevent CHD when made part of your moderate lifestyle.

As we all have different schedules and are psychologically different, no one plan of exercise is good for all. Like crash diets, a sporadic, on-again-off-again programme is not useful. Once you stop it ceases to do good. That's why you hear about athletes whose muscles turn to fat when they stop active sport. This isn't strictly true, but less exercise means less fat burned off, less muscle tone: therefore if you eat the same amount and don't burn it off, the excess accumulates in the body as fat.

The best plan would be to exercise all your muscles three or four times a week with stretching or light-weights plus a 30 minute aerobic plan – that is one which would get your blood pumping for 20 or more minutes at a steady rate, elevating it enough to allow your heart to strengthen and for the blood to flow to the parts that other activities cannot reach.

In addition to this exercise session you must become more aware of how you can exercise all the time and thus build up your heart and circulatory system. Your legs help to pump the blood around your body, that's why running is good for your heart – your secondary circulatory system will open up and develop with exercise. To illustrate the many different activities that will do the job I'll explain how I added exercise to my life!

Living in England doesn't offer us consistently good weather; try to plan an outdoor activity such as a picnic or a barbecue a week in advance! It's difficult enough to plan one for the same afternoon even if the sun is shining in the morning. Therefore I needed an aerobic exercise to do in the house, where I could be sure I would stick to a set routine. I chose an exercise bicycle. It is an excellent form of controlled cardiovascular exercise, but terribly boring – so I read and cycle.

'People are dying as a result of badly prescribed exercise and there should be laws against self-appointed fitness experts who have no idea of the dangers involved. The danger of death during exercise emphasises the need for extreme caution when prescribing programmes of vigorous leisure activity.'

Dr Bruce Davies, Dept of Human Kinetics at Salford
University

'350 executives, aged between 40 and 60, underwent
laboratory tests at Salford this year and abnormalities
were identified in 80 per cent of them. These included
irregular heart beat, high blood pressure and overweight.'

The Times. September, 1984

'A Sheffield reader writes: "Today I did the ABC Road
Test (two miles) in 32 minutes – eight days ago it took
me 50 minutes. I'm four stone overweight and haven't
done any exercise for over 20 years, I'm amazed at how
my body is responding".

Sunday Times Magazine, September, 16th, 1984 from
'Oliver Gillie answers readers' questions'.

Never do what that Sheffield reader did. Never plunge
into a strenuous activity when you are unfit and unused to
frequent and strenuous exercise. Also if you are overweight,
or smoke, or have not exercised for years, or are over 35
years old, or have other risk factors, you should not even
begin to do any strenuous exercise unless you have first
discussed the matter with your doctor. Exercise is important for an all-round health and fitness plan, but sudden
strenuous exercise may also mean sudden death!

You must check with your doctor as to the state of your
health to see what types of activity you shouldn't do.
Obviously an unfit person with many risk factors such as
high blood pressure, overweight and a family history of
heart disease should do less strenuous exercise than a
young person who is fit from playing sports in the past and
wants to develop an exercise programme because he has a
sedentary job. You must pick out an activity to suit you.

With cycling I can increase the pressure on my exercise cycle to make it harder to pedal. I can time it, and I can increase my rate of pedalling if I want – it allows me to control how hard I exercise and allows me to do it constantly for a set period of time. And I can do it at home.

Any type of aerobic exercise will do the job, and I don't mean just leaping up and down to disco music in a leotard. Swimming, cycling, brisk walking, running and jogging are perfect activities. Swimming is probably the best of all, as you exercise almost all your muscles in one activity, swim laps for endurance and at the same time aerobically exercise your heart. But the problem always seems to be getting to a pool three or four days a week. And in cold weather the idea can be daunting.

Climbing stairs and treadmill walking or jogging, rope skipping and running in place are also good. Competitive sports can be aerobic – such as handball, tennis, squash and football.

The object of aerobics is to elevate your pulse rate for short periods – making your heart beat faster and thereby strengthening it through mild exertion. It will then perform more efficiently at rest. This can be determined by touching any artery and counting the beats (pulse rate) – your wrist offers the easiest method. It measures heart-beat and is a guage that tells you how hard your body is working. A lower pulse means that the heart is resting between beats, filling your heart more slowly and providing the needed oxygen with less effort and more efficiency. Your pulse rate, at rest, will give you an idea of how hard your heart is working. Men average 72 to 76 beats per minute; women 75 to 80 beats a minute. Each person has a different normal pulse rate, and this would be up to your doctor to determine. But the lower your pulse rate, the healthier you should be. A resting pulse rate of more than 80 may indicate lack of fitness and that the heart is pumping harder than it should.

119

The period when you elevate your pulse rate (by exercise) should take it to 160 minus your age (if you are 45 it's 115) and keep it there for 20 minutes. This should be done gradually with a warm-up period before your activity and a cooling-down period afterwards.

My programme will illustrate what I mean:

1. I begin by doing some stretching exercises. My wife does yoga stretching exercises which really pull and stretch the muscles in your back, legs, arms and neck. I have picked out a few that I like to do.

2. Then I use light weights (10 pounds) and do a few strengthening exercises for my shoulders and stomach.

3. After this I do sit-ups to strengthen my stomach (I tend to put on weight around my waist and I have to exercise to keep that in check) and press-ups for muscle tone in my arms, chest and back. (This also elevates the pulse rate and isn't good for those of you who are not reasonably fit.)

4. I use my cycle at low load (75) for two minutes; at medium load (100) for three minutes; then fifteen minutes at a constant, taxing rate (125); and three minutes at 140 if I feel strong. Then I cool down at two minutes at 100, and two minutes at 75.

5. I then do another set of sit-ups and press-ups and I feel tired, but pleased with myself, physically fitter and relieved of the guilt I would have felt if I hadn't exercised.

If you lower your resting heart beat by five to ten beats a minute over a period of time you will have accomplished your goal.

Your programme should be progressive – that is, begin slowly and carefully and then progress, gradually increasing your activity to strengthen your body and heart. Always be *moderate*. Don't overdo the intensity of any activity to the point where it overstretches you, as you could pull a muscle, hurt your back or overstress your heart. There are deaths that happen on the squash courts, to joggers and even on golf courses. Some of them have happened to people who were doing more than they should have been doing for their personal condition. This must be assessed. I would like to introduce you to the fact that a moderate programme of exercise is needed in all our lives – you must find out for yourself the programme that is best for you personally.

If you get a pain in your chest – *stop*. It could be anything, but a pain in the chest is sometimes a warning signal, and you should see your doctor immediately if it happens while you are exercising, as physical stress might bring on symptoms of existing heart disease that mild activity can't reveal. (See Exercise Stress Test Page 68.)

There are ordinary activities that you can use to keep you fit. Once you become aware of your muscles from doing the stretching exercises, you will learn how to use them better. Simple lifting, if you tense the proper muscles can exercise you further. I have a posture problem – slouching – and when I stand up properly I can feel the muscles in my back and shoulders strengthening. This awareness makes me exercise these muscles when I walk normally.

Walking up stairs is good. I now tend to walk briskly, rather than leisurely as before – I use stairs to exercise my legs and heart. I especially like the long underground escalators. I walk up on the left and never stand quietly on the right. I never run up stairs, just walk – briskly. In fact, walking up stairs is good exercise as an activity but I've always found that I couldn't do it for a long period of time. I use it periodically to strengthen my legs. If I have a busy day and can't exercise then I try to compensate by using my daily activities instead. Walking briskly is good. Being aware of your physical exertion is good.

Certain non-aerobic activities are isometric. This means they tend to squeeze the blood out of some muscles rather than increasing the flow of blood to them and can be harmful if you are not really fit. Weightlifting and any very exerting activity can be harmful. Press-ups are not good, and any activity where you feel your temples pounding may not be good, as these isometric exercises tend to raise your blood pressure.

Carrying the groceries, moving furniture (but not if you have a back problem) and any physical daily activity will elevate your heart rate and make your overall body performance more efficient. This increased rate of activity burns up energy and calories. Once you develop a more active way of life, even walking short distances that you normally drive, or walking up the stairs rather than taking the lift, or walking around the room a few times with your arms full of groceries before putting them down, helps burn up calories. Sitting on the sofa, munching chocolates, crisps, or biscuits, doesn't.

Once you are age 35 or more, competitive sports are out unless you are fit and have your doctor's approval. The 'once a year' mile run or the football game are not wise. Those who begin to run or jog must remember not to overdo it. Never push yourself to the point of chest pain, nausea, fatigue or pains in your side – runner's burn is not good, unless you are in superb shape. There are many aerobic systems with point evaluations to monitor progress, but for now you must start a simple exercise programme and learn more about what the best system is for you. Remember *there is no easy way to fitness*, it takes time and sweat. Five or ten minutes a day will stretch or tone your muscles, but it will not help your heart, lungs or circulation very much.

Exercise:

● Exercise lowers Blood Pressure by dilating blood vessels in skin and muscles. It increases the pumping efficiency of your heart and as the heart becomes stronger it pumps more slowly and efficiently lowering heart rate.

- Exercise increases the opening and elasticity of coronary arteries as blood is pumped more strongly. Collateral arteries and blood vessels are opened with heavy physical activity and blood goes further in the circulatory system.
- Exercise also reduces stress by giving vent to pent-up physical and emotional anxieties and tension.
- Clotting mechanisms are beneficially affected because exercise stimulates the release of certain hormones and other chemicals into blood.
- Exercise chemically lowers blood fat level and may remove some fatty build-up inside the arteries.
- Blood transports oxygen to tissue, the brain, heart, lungs and muscles – exercise makes this activity more efficient.

THE MODERATION DIET

It is more than fifteen years since I found out that I had
CHD, and was in the highest risk section; those with the
inherited FH. I subsequently found out all I could about
the subject and realised that I had been leading the type of
life that was harmful to my health and was probably killing
me. Diseases of lifestyle caused by eating, drinking,
smoking, stress and polution have replaced the germ-
induced diseases of former years. But they kill just the same
and you cannot be inoculated against coronary heart
disease, strokes or heart attacks.

I realised that I had to change my lifestyle. I ate too
much in general and too many bad foods. I had a job that
created pressure which I found difficult to handle. my
personality was such that I created pressure for myself even
when there was none. Although I was enjoying an affluent
Californian lifestyle I was killing myself, or at least
allowing bad living habits to wear away at my body.

One word present in all the reports recommending
control of CHD is *moderation*. I recognised that my
approach to life was extreme. although enthusiastic. I
needed to control my excesses. to moderate my diet and my
reaction to things around me – and these past fifteen years
or so have been years spent creating my own lifestyle of
moderation.

I tried to eliminate extremes. I discovered the foods that
were bad in my diet and many of the foods that helped to
keep my body healthy. I realised that a strict crash diet
wouldn't work for me. as I craved certain foods and I was

124

reluctant to eliminate them from my life. I also realised that once I stopped adhering to a 'crash diet' I would go back to all my bad habits (as most people do) and put on the weight again. So I decided that if I were serious (and I was because I knew that I was heart attack prone and I didn't want to die) I would have to moderate my life style, and I did.

The normal British diet is very different from the diet man ate thousands of years ago. We were genetically adapted for another way of life. Professor Geoffrey Rose points out that we need to restore our own biological normality. The best way to achieve this is by removing any unnatural factors such as excess dietary fats and smoking, rather than by introducing other unnatural substances to our bodies – such as a high intake of drugs. A moderate lifestyle change is preferable.

I often notice people on trains and buses unwrap a bar of chocolate and eat the whole thing. For them eating sweets and biscuits has become a habit and second nature – a *bad* habit that is passed on to their children. In pubs I see pint after pint of fattening beer being downed along with pies and sausages containing enormous proportions of fat as well as crisps and pork pies and steak and chips. All of these foods may be eaten – but not in the daily quantities that for many are a 'way of life'. Looking around me I see that most people are still doing what I did in 1968. They are ignoring all the information that is readily available to them now – all the knowledge based upon research into how to avoid heart attacks – and they act as if it doesn't concern them.

I haven't cut out all the goodies from my diet. I eat everything – but now in moderation. I know what foods are bad for me and I look upon them as treats and still enjoy them – but less often. I like wine, beer, good scotch and port, and the occasional cigar. But I keep it all within my self-set limits. I have undergone most of the tests to assess the damage I have done to my coronary system and I visit my doctor regularly as part of my plan for survival.

Once you have damaged your health, a clock begins to tick a countdown – a bomb within yourself. It is up to you to slow that ticking down. The answers are all around us, if only we'd listen and follow the advice of medical science. I look upon bad foods as poison. When I do eat something that I know is bad for me I use the guilt that follows to force me to eat far less than I would have normally – and I savour the small amounts I allow myself to have.

When I was younger I played sports just for fun and pleasure; I now endure my daily exercises and exercise bicycle with intense boredom and sometimes pain. But I know the alternative, and I prefer to follow the programme. I certainly feel a sense of achievement once I've done it.

The next sections explain how you can create a programme that will work for you, with the help of your willpower and your will to survive and your desire to live a healthier life. And you'll look better too!

A HEALTHY DIET AND NUTRITION

What we are fed as children will form our eating habits for life – our food cravings and our pet hates. I have a friend who adores sago pudding – I don't know anyone else who does, but I'm sure there are those of you who may. He is allowed sago soufflée on his birthday as there is no one in his family who would watch him eat it any other day of the year. He eats it with tinned pears. Another friend, who understands nutrition and has enjoyed eating in luxurious restaurants and homes, when eating alone will devour a plate of white bread and chocolate spread.

No matter how sophisticated our acquired tastes become, our food cravings remain basic. I can't imagine waking up at three in the morning and thinking I'd give anything for grouse and a bottle of Petrus '61. I'm more likely to crave a fried egg sandwich, a few sausages and chips, a chocolate bar or a hunk of creamy cake, a sticky bun or pastry.

As my childhood was spent in Brooklyn, New York, my theme song could be 'I left my heart in Coney Island', which is something like the Blackpool of New York. The smell of hot dogs and hamburgers, french fried potatoes, and the cool taste of soft ice-cream, cold milk and chocolate cake is etched into my psyche. My youth was spent devouring quantities of foods high in fats and cholesterol and great flavour. The line between a food being a culinary delight or an adult pacifier is a thin one, so we must curb our excessive passions for the psychologically instantly satisfying foods. I can picture myself after playing a game of baseball, standing with the fridge door open, drinking milk from a quart bottle, oreo biscuits (chocolate creams) five or ten at a sitting, or eating chocolate ice-cream out of the half-gallon carton. This memory alone sends my blood pressure and blood cholesterol levels soaring.

There is such a strong addiction to chocolate in any form, in my family that I'm certain that our DNA must contain the special 'Adler gene', which is an inherited craving for chocolate.

Moderation Diet: Eat *less* – substitute good for bad. Simplistic – but effective.

True I was overweight, and I needed to lose weight permanently. I knew that friends of ours who dieted always seemed to put the weight back on, and my problem was simply eating too much (quantity), and choosing bad, rather than good foods (quality). The simple approach I followed, and still do, is *eat less*, which means smaller amounts of all foods at each sitting; cut out second portions wherever possible; cut down on snacks and the habit of reaching for a biscuit or a sandwich when you need a break or oral gratification. I learned what was bad for me and substituted good wherever possible.

Some crash diets will have you either drinking huge amounts of water or juices, or eating pineapple or other foods not normally found in our diets – and/or depriving you of the foods you are used to or particularly enjoy. I decided not to eliminate anything I like – I simply ate half the amount. Where I normally would eat four biscuits with a cup of tea, I cut back to two (now I have one); where I'd eat four sausages, I'd have two; and I wouldn't have a second hamburger. I substituted a small order of fries for a large one and I'd started to leave some. I realised that I spent quite a lot of time eating from other people's plates. I no longer allowed myself this lack of discipline – I needed to learn to account to myself for everything I ate.

Therefore, to change your way of eating – your habits of a lifetime – don't eliminate the foods you enjoy, just eat less of them – smaller portions and less often. Be aware that they are not good for you and that they are now a treat.

UNDERSTANDING FAT

I found the subject of fat very confusing and I would be surprised if you understood it. Calories are energy; an accepted measurement for energy consumed in our food and used through activity, or burned up during exercise. Some foods are high in bulk and low in calories for their weight so you can eat more of them for the same amount of calories. Fats are the highest calorie food of all. Sugar at 112 calories an ounce is better than butter and all kinds of margarines at 210 calories an ounce – and vegetable oils and cooking fats are 255 calories an ounce. So you see why slimming diets recommend you grill rather than fry. All fats are 100 per cent fat, which includes the polyunsaturated margarines, the sunflower margarines and the vegetable

128

margarines and oils and butter – each will give you the same number of calories per portion or ounce.

However, although they are equal when it comes to calories and putting on weight, or losing it, they are far from equal when it comes to the question of cholesterol and coronary heart disease. The amount of *saturated* fats in the foods determines whether they are bad for your heart. Polyunsaturated fat is recommended at a proportion of two to one over saturated fats, and the question is not one of low-fat margarine, but what percentage of saturated fats does it contain? There are hidden fats (both saturated and other fats) in many foods such as cheese, milk, pastries, chocolate, crisps and many convenience, packaged and canned foods. Hence the need for proper labelling of foods to inform us of the fat percentages. Once you are aware of the total fat content in the foods that you eat and aware of the saturated fat content as well, you can begin to make decisions to balance your diet, either to lose or gain weight – or for a healthier heart.

Fat provides more than 40 per cent of dietary energy (calories) in Great Britain. It needs to be reduced to 28–30 per cent of food energy.

Dairy products – milk, butter, cream, cheese – supply 31 per cent of all our fat and 41 per cent of all our saturated fat.

Percentage of calories as fat:

silver-top milk – 52 per cent
full fat yoghurt – 52 per cent
sausages – 70 per cent
butter *or* margarine – 100 per cent
Cheddar cheese – 71 per cent
bacon – 60–80 per cent
red meat – 55–75 per cent
(the extra 20 per cent is the fat you trim off)

There has been no reduction of fat consumption in this country in the last ten years or more. Fat was 40 per cent of food energy in 1974 and was 41 per cent in 1982 – and plasma cholesterol concentrations may still be rising.

WHAT CAN YOU DO?

Almost every report suggests that we reduce our total fat intake from 40 to 30 per cent of our daily calories. Learn how to balance your food intake – to substitute lower fat, lower caloried foods for the higher fat foods – you will help your heart and lose weight in the process. If you don't want to, or don't need to lose weight, then you can learn to maintain your present weight by eating a healthier diet. Moderation does not mean less pleasure from eating.

I started by eating more foods lower in fats such as chicken, fish, vegetables and fruits, skimmed milk – and eating less of red meats, butter, cream, milk, cheese, fried foods, and sausages. You will need to increase your ratio of vegetable protein to animal protein.

Once the food industry supplies us with full labelling of the nutritional contents of each packaged food (i.e. the saturated and other fats, sugar, salt and fibre) then we should be able to choose our food properly, according to its nutritional value not just its tempting package.

The next section will tell you about nutrition in general and specifically what is good and bad for your heart and arteries. You can then begin to eat less of the bad and start substituting the good in your daily diet.

FOOD – THE GOOD, THE BAD AND THE TASTY

We are usually influenced to buy products we see advertised on television and in magazines, and in some cases we are sold institutions rather than just brand names. We see advertisements for BP, British Telecom, Pure New Wool, electricity, New Zealand lamb, French apples. Some of the eating habits we have acquired were programmed by advertising campaigns that have successfully put nutritional ideas into our lives that are not quite valid. Most of us feel that milk in large quantities is good for babies, and that a chubby baby is adorable; that butter is better; that cream is naughty but nice; that an apple a day will keep the doctor away and we should drink a pinta milk a day.

We now know that saturated fats are bad for us because they raise our blood cholesterol level, and that polyunsaturated fats are better for us as they are thought to reduce the blood cholesterol caused by animal fats in a ratio of two to one. For example, one teaspoonful of corn oil will cancel out the saturated fat of $\frac{1}{2}$ teaspoon of bacon fat. But remember: *all* fats, saturated or not, are still 100 per cent fat and very high in calories.

MILK

Moderation diet: Avoid full fat milk, use skimmed milk. Semi-skimmed milk contains less than 2 per cent fat skimmed milk contains less than 0.1 per cent fat.

Milk has the purest image of all, as mother's milk is often the first food we know and drinking milk is encouraged from childhood.

Milk supplies about 13 per cent of the fat in the British diet and 17 per cent of saturated fat in our food intake.

Silver top full cream milk contains 3.3 per cent protein, 3.8 per cent fats and 87 per cent water.

Milk does contain important vitamins and minerals, but it also has large amounts of saturated fats and cholesterol. Gold-top is the worst culprit: the creamier the milk the worse it is for you. Skimmed milk is fine, it has all the nutrition without the fat. Unfortunately it is thinner and has less flavour and texture than fuller cream milks, but again, once you get used to it you wonder how you ever drank any other kind.

131

When we lived in Brazil and Spain we didn't have the same problem that we have in England. There the milk was thin and tasted like chalk. Therefore we drank less of it. In Britain the cream is the best in the world and the dairy products, in their pure state, are unrivaled anywhere – but they should be considered luxuries for those of us who need to eat a lower saturated fat diet.

Just a note about coffee whiteners (also called substitute creamers.) They are no substitutes for milk – you're better off sticking with milk. They are made of glucose, vegetable oils and milk solids – approximately 34 per cent fat and 98 per cent of that fat is saturated fat.

Skimmed milk is the best, semi-skimmed (far more fat than skimmed, but half that of full-cream milk) is next. Try a mixture at first, or substitute the semi-skimmed for the milk you now take and try gradually to substitute skimmed for normal milk. This includes putting it on your cereal, in cooking, baking and in puddings. Skimmed milk has all the nutritional value, without the fats and calories. Its value to your health cannot be underestimated. Therefore I mix my bran with a toasted, honey-added bran and although I increase the calories somewhat, I can still tolerate eating the bran which is very important. I drink only skimmed milk and have done for over ten years, and now find the taste of the cream in milk offensive.

FACT:
Skimming the fat from the milk leaves all the proteins, minerals and most of the vitamins. But 90 per cent of all milk drunk in Great Britain is full-fat.

CREAM

Cream in any form, is high in saturated fat and should be avoided. Cream is to be considered a treat and you should not eat cream cakes or pour cream over puddings as a habit – remember that it is something special to be enjoyed infrequently. I know that it's hard if you enjoy your strawberries with thick, rich cream. Savour it when you have it – but have it less often. Cream is also very high in fats and calories, so you will be doing both your heart and your image in the mirror a favour if you cut down on the amount you eat.

EGGS

Moderation Diet: Egg yolks are high in saturated fats. You should limit them to three a week if you are concerned about your saturated fat and cholesterol level.

Eggs have the image of being cheap and nutritious and we are encouraged to eat them frequently and in large quantities. The yolk of the egg has one of the highest concentrations of cholesterol and saturated fats of any food. The egg white has zero cholesterol and fat and is rich in protein, vitamins and minerals. The yolk is high in fat and calories. You can eat as many egg whites as you like – the yolks are not good for your health if you have a CHD problem.

Therefore, reduce your egg consumption to three a week and remember you must also count the eggs you cook and bake with. Recipes using whites are better than those for yolks. Cutting down on eggs is only one way to reduce the saturated fat in your diet, but you must remember that eggs can't be eaten indiscriminately – even athletes now control the amount of eggs they eat. The steak and six eggs breakfast is no longer encouraged for weightlifters.

CHEESES

Moderation Diet: Full-fat cheeses such as cheddar are bad. Low fat cheeses are good.

133

Avoid the full fat cheeses such as Cheddar, Stilton, Danish Blue and cream cheeses – they are treats to be eaten for pleasure and enjoyed, but much less often than you eat them now. Substitute other cheeses such as Edam, Camembert, or cottage or curd cheese (made from skimmed milk). If you are a cheese lover study the chart (page 170) and start to eat those lower in fat content.

Try not to add cream to your coffee, and remember ice-cream may be rich in cream – however some low fat ice-cream and sorbets may not be. Low fat yoghurts are fine, but avoid the creamier, thicker, richer yoghurts. Read the labels and select those made with skimmed milk.

BUTTER

Moderation Diet: Butter supplies 12 per cent of all the fats we eat and 16 per cent of the saturated fat in our daily diet. You should use it moderately – only as a treat.

Butter is not better when it concerns cholesterol, as it consists of 60 per cent saturated fats, a very large percentage, and although it tastes good to most of us it should be used as a treat. You don't have to cut it out completely (unless your doctor advises you to do so) but you should substitute margarines or oils that are low in saturated fat, both on your bread and in cooking. We use far more butter than we need to out of habit. Whenever you use butter just remember that it is bad and see if you can substitute all or part of the amount you use with something that is better for you. If you use butter half as often you are accomplishing a lot. But read the labels carefully on so-called substitutes – they may use vegetable oils that are very high in saturated fats, and a low-fat spread may be high in saturated fats.

MARGARINES

Moderation Diet: Margarines are made with different fats and oils, some with palm, coconut oil, or lard, all high in saturated fats. Once again the one lowest in saturated fats and highest in polyunsaturated fats is best.

All spreads and oils contain fats, therefore all are high in calories and are fattening, so you should start to limit the amount and frequency of their use in your diet. I now use less on bread and no longer put butter or margarine on vegetables – I add lemon or herbs instead. Margarines labelled 'high in polyunsaturates' are the ones to use. Others may be high in saturated fats – and it is difficult to tell from the labelling which are better than others. Try to stick with those 'high in polyunsaturated fats' and use as sparingly as possible.

COOKING AND SALAD OILS

Moderation Diet: Saturated fats tend to get hard at room temperature, so soft margarines and oils are usually better.

Don't buy oils labelled vegetable oil, unless they state which oils they contain.

Don't use lard or dripping. Use corn oil or other oils low in saturated fat.

Avoid the use of lard, suet, dripping, cooking oils and vegetable oils where the type of oil isn't clearly stated on the label, especially oils of 'unknown origin' which could be from old Spanish gear-boxes for all we know. Cooking oils clearly illustrate the difference between the categories of fats. Corn oil, safflower oil, sunflower oil, soya oil, and wheatgerm oil are mixtures of saturated and poly-

135

unsaturated fats in safe proportions. These are recommended for cooking and salads. Peanut oil and olive oil are
monosaturated fats but they don't have the value of those
listed above which contain 50 per cent or more polyunsaturates. They are not as bad however as the oils high in
saturated fats (the animal fats such as lard, and other
vegetable oils such as coconut and palm oil). Coconut is
one of those vegetable products very high in saturated fats,
like chocolate and avocados.

As labelling is difficult to assess, try to mix your own
salad dressing unless a prepared dressing states the fat
content (page 163) and remember to use any oil or salad
dressing sparingly, as they all contain fats and calories.

Moderation Diet: If you must fry, use corn oil.

Foods cooked in oils, especially fried foods, are not a
good idea especially if we don't know the type of fat that
was used. As my wife is from Yorkshire, I learned that the
tastiest Yorkshire puddings are baked in dripping and the
best fish and chips are cooked in lard. Settle for second best
– cook your chips in corn oil (if you must eat chips at all,
and if you are like me you *must* occasionally). Packets of
crisps are not only fattening but high in saturated fats from
the cooking oils – so cut down, eat half a packet and put
some aside.

Packaged cakes and biscuits provide 6 per cent of the
total fat and 6.6 per cent of saturated fat in British diet.

Filled biscuits are usually made with palm and coconut
oils, both highly saturated. The simpler the biscuit the
better.

Packaged cakes and biscuits and puddings present a
problem, as do any products inside a can or packet where
the fat content is not clearly stated. All biscuits and cakes
are made with fat and milk; the question is what kind of
fat? Of course you must cut down on quantity as that is the
best way to reduce the fat intake, but try to avoid creamy

cakes or sponges with creamy centres or those that are rich in butter, eggs and milk.

Now for something good about fats:
- they carry vitamins A, D, E, and K into the body
- they keep the skin healthy
- they keep us from getting hungry straight after a meal.

MEAT

Moderation Diet: Eat less red meat. Cut away all visible fat.

Not only is meat a very expensive part of the diet, but it is high in saturated fats – both visible and invisible. The first rule in eating red meats is to cut off all the visible fats – and never cook fatty meats. Lean cuts of meat are more expensive, therefore eat smaller portions and less often.

We all know what fat looks like: it is thick, yellowish-white and greasy and is poison for your heart. It collects inside the arteries and kills. Eliminate as much as possible from your diet. If you stop fat from passing your lips it can't get into your arteries. The British diet is filled with fatty foods that we are encouraged to eat – streaky bacon and sausages are some of the worst, as are meat pies and pasties that have a high fat content (and most do). The meat producers must be encouraged, and possibly forced, to use less fat in their products. The legal requirements are very lenient. Certain products that contain a large proportion of saturated fats are clearly dangerous to your health and if they don't carry a health warning, at least they should state how much fat they contain.

Beef and lamb are high in fats, as is pork. Try not to eat crackling – it is almost pure fat. Ham, lean mince and other meats with the fat cut off are acceptable, but should be eaten in smaller quantities. All offal – liver, kidneys and brains are very high in cholesterol, although some offal may also be high in minerals such as iron. Once again cut down, if not out.

SAUSAGES

Moderation Diet: Sausages are high in saturated fat – *eat less.*

If you must eat sausages (and I must) eat those with a high meat content, and eat less of them. The British banger contains bread as well as meat and other ingredients such as bone, offal and intestine. The meat content may be stated, but read the label carefully. It is confusing – for our sakes it should be required to state the fat content in sausages as well as the meat content. At present, where the meat content is stated, this may include more fat than lean meat. What we must look for is the fat content, which is not easy to find. So just assume that sausages are filled with fat unless you know the contents. Eat them sparingly – no need to cut them out entirely but always remember they are bad for your heart.

BACON

Moderation Diet: Streaky bacon is bad. Eat less fatty cuts such as back bacon and lean gammon. Cut excess visible fat away. In sausages 70 per cent of the calories (energy) is fat – in bacon, salami, frankfurters and paté it is 80 per cent.

You can easily see the fat on bacon. More expensive back bacon has less fat. Streaky bacon, though tasty has more fat. Eat less bacon and when you do eat it try more expensive cuts. Once again start by eating two strips of bacon rather than four and then one instead of two. I like bacon sandwiches but I have them as an occasional treat and then I always use best back bacon. Now I break off all the visible fat after cooking and I eat two pieces where I used to eat four or five. Meat pies, sausage rolls, Cornish pasties, patés and meat paste, meat soups, pork pies, hamburgers and frankfurters are all bad for your heart. I eat them, but only occasionally and sparingly, and with a certain degree of guilt from the knowledge that they hurt rather than help. You needn't eliminate them completely – eat fewer and less often.

Fatty tinned meats such as luncheon meats, and pork are bad. Salami, garlic sausage, ham and other sausage preparations for sandwiches are bad. I eat them all, but far less than I used to.

POULTRY

> *Moderation Diet:* Don't eat chicken skin
> Chicken skin is 17 per cent fat
> Dark meat is 6 per cent fat
> White meat is 3 per cent fat
> Grill where possible – if you must fry, avoid deep frying.

Poultry such as chicken and turkey is good (but not the skin and the visible fat) and game and rabbit have less fat than red meat. But fatty poultry such as duck and goose is as bad as fatty red meat, and should be considered a treat for Christmas and special occasions. Always cut off the fat. I love Peking Duck and I haven't given it up. It has just become a treat. I've learned to enjoy some of the vegetable dishes at Chinese and Indian restaurants.

FISH

Fish is generally good (see table page 167) except for fish roe and caviare. Some fish are less fatty than others, such as white fish, whiting, haddock, cod and sole. Oily fish such as herring, mackerel, salmon, tuna and sardines contain a lot of polyunsaturated fats. Shellfish such as shrimp and prawns are low in fats. although high in cholesterol, and should only be eaten occasionally – and in Great Britain most of us only eat these expensive foods rarely.

SPREADS

As most spreads are mixtures of different substances. some animal. vegetable and chemical. it is difficult to determine how much fat and cholesterol is in each spread, and what harm it does. in what quantity. Patés are usually fatty and bad for you. as are many liver and ham spreads and meat and fish pastes – they should be eaten in moderation. Mayonnaise is made from oil and egg yolks, so it should be used sparingly. It is part of my life as I enjoy tuna salad with celery and mayonnaise (from my childhood) but there are now some mayonnaises with polyunsaturated fats. I prefer the other kind. but I have cut down on the amount I eat.

Sweet spreads are not good for you as both chocolate and peanut butter are high in cholesterol and fat.

FIBRE. CEREALS AND GRAINS

We know that fibre is good for us. But why? Fibre is a name given to a whole range of plant substances. that pass right through the intestines without being absorbed into the body. Their value is that they provide roughage and aid digestion. Fibre also prevents too much fat and sugar getting into the bloodstream too quickly. It binds bile salts in the gut and in the bowel. thus reducing the amount of cholesterol which can be absorbed in the system. Fibre in our diet comes mainly from bread, cereals, potatoes, pulses, leafy vegetables and fruit – with their skins whenever possible. No animal or dairy products contain fibre. Beans, lentils and bran have a high fibre content. Wholegrain cereals and wholegrain bread, unrefined flours and grains such as corn and brown rice are very

140

good for you. Fibre has finally made it. Books, the media and doctors have helped to make dietary fibre and bran household words in the UK. Supermarkets now offer a variety of wholemeal alternatives to white bread and flour. I must confess to liking a white sesame roll with a hamburger (especially at barbecues) and croissants and brioche have been counted among my weaknesses. But wholemeal bread is a basic part of my diet. Croissants and fancy breads and crackers have lots of high saturated fats, salt and sugar – so remember it is not just the white flour in bread and pastries that is bad.

Great Britain is a constipated nation. The British diet lacks sufficient fibre such as that found in vegetables and fruit, beans and wholegrain cereals, oatmeal, sweetcorn, brown rice, lentils and nuts. We eat too much white flour and white bread, and even the standard brown loaf lacks sufficient fibre (wholegrain or wholemeal bread is best). We overcook our vegetables and eat more rich pastries, puddings, fried foods, crisps and sweets than are healthy for us. Once again it's the quantity eaten that matters. Be *moderate*: eat less of these foods and begin to substitute high fibre foods in small amounts.

Your daily calories and your money are better spent on high fibre. High bulk foods such as wholegrain bread, brown rice, pasta, potatoes, fruits and vegetables. They are high in carbohydrates, but carbohydrates are lighter in calories than fat. Obviously eating too much of almost anything will increase your caloric intake, but you're far better off eating foods that are low in fats – all fats. For example, if you eat a piece of bread (wholemeal or white, even though the wholemeal has far more nutritional value) the butter or margarine you spread on it is almost all fat and very heavy in calories, whereas the jam, though almost all sugar, contains little or no fat. Therefore if you spread on less butter or margarine and add a little jam instead, you will benefit from the fact that sugar at 122 calories an ounce is one-half the calories of the butter.

Pasta and potatoes are high in carbohydrates and fibre (especially potatoes cooked in their skins, either baked or boiled); it's the sauce that you add that can be a problem. A fresh tomato sauce with a little cheese – no meat – is terrific. Try it with herbs or vegetables, it's fine. It's when you add fat that the problem begins. Cooking minced beef or onions or peppers, in butter or oil (even if the oil is safflower) results in a dish high in calories. Don't put a large blob of margarine or butter on the potatoes, be restrained – it's those fats, not the potatoes, you need to be more careful with. It seems that some sugared cereals may contain as much nutritional value as sugared cardboard. If you crave them have them – but infrequently. Try un-sugared bran cereals. Bran-based and wholegrain cereals are very high in fibre. But be sure to check the labels of cereals for their salt and sugar contents as some are much higher than others. Fibre is present in vegetables, fruits and other foods. Oatmeal, wholegrain cereals and breads, all breads made with wholemeal flour (try to avoid butter), wholegrain rice (brown rice), and wholegrain pasta (dark in colour rather than white) all are high in fibre and nutrition. White rice is less acceptable as are white pasta, and sugar-coated breakfast cereals.

If you must persist with your favourite cereal, use skimmed milk with it. When eating rice or pasta don't have butter, use a sauce made with polyunsaturated oil or serve it with margarine or vegetables rather than with meat – that way you are moderating your eating habits. It's the constant diet of bad foods that causes problems. You can break the chain by substituting some good for some bad – there's no need to give up eating all your favourite foods.

A hot croissant with butter and jam, or a scone with cream and jam is obviously not good for you – but if you must have it, eat one where you used to have two. Eat half, instead of a whole; cut down on the amount of jam and substitute margarine for butter. Or use half butter, half margarine. It's a start, and if you get results with this diet – that is if your blood cholesterol level is reduced to normal, you need not go to extremes in your eating pattern. *Moderation* may be the answer. *How* moderate is for you to find out.

Please remember that by example we pass on our bad eating habits to our children. Spend more time choosing the healthiest type of food for your family. The way to better health can be pleasurable and not a torture. Strict diets are a form of torture and usually unnatural to the way we like to eat – that's why no one finds it easy or fun sticking to a diet. Eating well should and can be a pleasant way to live – and to live longer.

FRUIT AND VEGETABLES

All fresh fruits and vegetables are good, as are frozen ones. Foods high in fibre are especially good such as sweet corn, peas, beans, lentils, and potatoes with their skins. Green vegetables and salads are excellent with the exception of avocados, coconuts and olives.

DRINKS

Alcohol in excess is bad and tea, coffee and fruit juices are better. Remember that too much caffeine isn't good for you and soft drinks, tea and coffee contain caffeine. I now drink decaffeinated coffee as I found the ordinary kind irritated my stomach and I find it just as satisfying. Therefore I've cut down on tea, and drink more fruit juices, mineral water and diet drinks.

SWEETS AND DESSERTS

Milk or creamed puddings, dairy ice-cream, pastry puddings, cakes, biscuits and sauces (such as custard) made with milk or cream, eggs or unsuitable fat or oils, are bad, as are most proprietary puddings and sauces. All you need to do is to cut down on the quantity because life wouldn't be the same without them. Be aware that fresh fruit or other less fatty desserts are better and start to substitute or cut down. Most tinned fruits are very high in sugar. But remember there's no point in having strawberries or bananas if you pour a huge dollop of double cream on top. It's all part of educating yourself and your palate as well as your appetite.

SALT

Foods such as meat, bacon, sausages, butter, tinned vegetables, bread and cereals all contain salt. It is also a bad habit to sprinkle salt on foods. An excessive intake of salt may cause high blood pressure and we consume far too much of it. All health reports recommend that our intake of salt be reduced by half.

SUGAR

We get calories and energy from natural sugar in fresh fruits and vegetables. Most processed sweets and desserts contain sugar. Sugar has little nutritional value other than energy. Sugar can make you fat and possibly, for some, raise triglyceride level. Don't add sugar to foods and try to eliminate it from coffee and tea, or if you must, use artificial sweeteners. Sugar products such as glucose and lactose are promoted as a quick source of energy. Sugar is rapidly absorbed, it gives you a burst of energy. Excess is then removed from the blood and stored as fat. This high energy level does not last very long and the body then craves more of the same. Natural sugar such as that in fresh fruit, is released more slowly than that in sweet desserts.

THE WAY TO A BALANCED DIET – A SUMMARY

Our greatest problem is that we tend to eat far too much of one type of ingredient in our diet. We need fats, carbohydrates and protein – but not an excess of any one thing. Our two goals are to achieve a healthy heart and clear arteries and a healthy weight that we stick to, one that we feel good at and at which we look our best. Too much food in general and too much of any one type is bad.

1. Ideally your caloric intake should equal the energy you burn. If you are overweight, you need to eat less and exercise more. No crash diets or fad food regimes.

2. Eat less animal fats and proteins. Try to substitute vegetable protein (beans/grains) for animal protein (meats and dairy food). Eat smaller portions as our diet is already rich in protein. We need 40 gm of protein a day – half vegetable and half animal protein. 20 gm of animal protein is contained in 100 gm of lean meat – less than 4 oz steak.

3. The way you cook your food is also important. Grill, roast or bake rather than fry. Dripping and fat from meat contain saturated fat, so avoid using in gravy and don't save it for cooking – use polyunsaturated oil instead. Skim the fat from your stock *before* you make gravy. Use yoghurt as a sauce thickener.

4. Cut away all visible fat from meat and don't eat the skin of chicken, duck or turkey, or crackling.

5. Keep to about 3–4 eggs per week. Avoid liver, kidney and brains – all offal, including tripe, should be eaten in moderation.

6. Avoid animal shortening such as lard, suet and butter and hard margarines. Use polyunsaturated margarines and oils such as corn and safflower oil.

7. Avoid commercial fillings for meat pies, fruit pies, cake mixes, glazes and fillings as they contain the wrong type of fats and oils.

8. Avoid mayonnaise and creamy dressings for salad, use oil (polyunsaturated corn oil) or olive oil (which is neutral) and vinegar.

9. Use skimmed milk or semi-skimmed milk rather than full fat pasteurized. The less cream content the better.

10. Avoid sour cream, cream cheese and other high fat cheeses such as cheddar.

11. Don't add salt to food.

12. Avoid excess sugar in foods and drinks. Cut down on sweets, chocolate, biscuits, ice-cream and puddings. Don't always add custard or cream to puddings. They are treats, not an everyday indulgence.

13. Instead of white bread and white flour try to substitute wholemeal breads, wholegrain flour with a high bran content.

14. Eat wholegrain cereals, brown rice, beans, peas, carrots, green leaf vegetables, fresh fruit and potatoes with their skins.

15. Try to eat standard meals at set times – three a day. Avoid snacks, unless eating small amounts throughout the day is your normal eating pattern. Have low fat snacks such as celery, carrot sticks, fruits, rather than crisps and creamy buns. Eliminate the British breakfast as a habit. Eat more wholegrain high bran cereals, toast, fruit.

16. Don't add cream to your tea or coffee, use skimmed or semi-skimmed milk. Cut down on sugar, use artificial sweeteners if necessary. Dairy creamers or substitutes are very high in saturated fats and you're better off using any form of milk.

Although it is common sense that in order to lose weight we have to eat less than the energy we burn, few of us fully understand the concept. To put it into perspective; 100 calories of energy is burned up by nineteen minutes brisk walking or ten minutes of jogging. One slice of bread with butter is more than 100 calories.

The British diet is too high in calories and the way of life is too low in exercise. To give you an idea of how easy it is to put on weight with small insignificant foods, such as that packet of crisps, a bar of chocolate, two biscuits, etc., I mentioned that a slice of bread and butter is 100 calories. If you eat only 100 calories a day more than you burn up, you will gain ten and a half pounds in a year. Think about that one.

The following foods contribute 90 per cent of the saturated fat in the national diet. The simplest example of the kind of diet that is required is to reduce by half the intake of the foods that constitute 90 per cent of the saturated fat in the national diet. They are: milk and cream; cheese, butter, margarine (for saturated content); cooking fats, meat and meat products (excluding poultry); biscuits.

A loss of 20 pounds in four months can be achieved by lowering your caloric intake by 400 calories, combined with 30 minutes daily of brisk walking. It takes a bit of doing and strong discipline. That's why I decided that in order to lose weight permanently (with fluctuations of three to five pounds) I preferred to change my diet by eating less fatty food and less food in general, and I would exercise regularly. This seems to keep me in shape and is exactly what is needed to fight coronary disease.

Each of you must find a moderate diet, exercise and lifestyle plan that is good for you. The basic facts and rules are simple and the same for all of us. Good nutrition applies to everyone and an awareness of calories and fat content is necessary as a basis for good diet. Each person must learn to understand what his/her body needs. In my case I needed to put an emphasis on a low fat diet, needed to lose weight and to discover a daily exercise programme that would fit in with my family life and the English climate. I also needed to take a resin that would help my body to get rid of the excess cholesterol that was building up in my blood and inside my arteries.

In your case, and in that of each member of your family, the needs may be different – one may be overweight, another may need to gain weight. One family member may have a high cholesterol problem, others not. But in general the principles of a good healthy diet are universal and simple. Some members of the family may need to be more strict than others. I use margarine which is high in polyunsaturated fats but my wife and my daughter have no cholesterol problem and prefer a different type of margarine. They avoid butter except as a treat on special occasions, such as my wife's bread pudding, which is marvellous. But we all eat brown bread and cereal, have fibre in our diet and avoid eating too much meat, not because we are health food fanatics, but because healthy eating is a way of life.

THE BRITISH BREAKFAST – THE WAY TO START YOUR DAY TO SHORTEN YOUR LIFE

Like all those who stand up and proclaim the virtues of the good old traditional British Breakfast, I love it, but it is a love-hate relationship. British Rail can't discontinue it, and I can't resist it.

If anything symbolises the evils of the British diet it is eggs, bacon, sausage and chips, fried bread – everything fried in fat, with enough cholesterol to make controlling your intake impossible for the entire day.

It can be a treat; once in a while, but with many people it is a habit to eat all that greasy food first thing in the morning. If you must have a fry-up any time of the day (I'm always tempted by the smell of bacon cooking) have half of what you would normally eat; one egg, one strip of bacon, one sausage, one piece of bread, (with margarine, not fried or buttered) and cook in polyunsaturated fat. And if you must have a fried British breakfast have it as a treat once a week, (once a month would be even better). If you crave it more often, begin with a bowl of high-fibre cereal and skimmed milk – the price of your guilt, but probably the least expensive part of the meal. In the beginning treat it as a guilt offering, and then gradually eliminate the rest of the fried cholesterol and develop a sensible way to start the day.

THE BUSINESSMAN'S LUNCH – GUARANTEED TO KILL YOU BEFORE YOU REACH THE TOP

Along with the company car and health insurance (which you'll be glad you have if you keep eating and living the way you do), comes the lunch perk. This is often an excuse to overeat and drink for 'business reasons', and can be dangerous when granted to the greedy or those of us with bad dietary habits (that probably includes most of us). Prawn cocktail with mayonnaise, and steak and chips, and of course Black Forest gateau which was probably invented by Hitler in World War II to kill off the British population so that he wouldn't need to invade! There are other foods on the menu which may not immediately satisfy your lunchtime cravings but which are far better for you, such as; grilled fish, chicken (not in sauce), salad (no mayonnaise) fresh fruit (strawberries, no cream) fresh vegetables. Come on, make a start: cut out the chips and creamy desserts. And you will appreciate the new, svelte you.

While we are at it, lets cut down on the alcohol intake – it's bad for your waistline, your driving and your work.

Don't be part of the self-destructive fabric of our society, if not for your own sake for the sake of your family. Start to do some of the basic, everyday things that *really* save your life. Stop smoking, start exercising and remember to fasten your seat belt.

SCHOOL DINNERS – FOOD POISONING FOR CHILDREN

A five year survey carried out for the Inner London Education Authority by Surrey University showed that London's school meals are nutritionally ten years out of date.

The American Health Foundation found that cholesterol levels are too high in American children (average level is 160 mg per 100 millilitres – ideal level is only 110 mg). It should be reduced to lower the risk of later heart attacks. A related study of children in New York showed that much of the excessive saturated fat and cholesterol in the children's diets resulted from eating too many red meats and dairy products.

WHO IS RESPONSIBLE FOR NUTRITION?

A nutrition education reinforced by a good diet is the way to begin to solve the British bad diet problem. Ideally we should start with the young, by providing them with school meals that are healthy and teaching them to eat the foods that are good for them. Of course we know that children love chocolate, fish fingers and chips, sausages and ice-cream – but they're no different from the rest of us – in the school canteen of our minds we are still children. We developed habits then that we are fighting to break now.

I fail to understand how a system that has nutritionists on its staff could poison our children with foods high in fats, sugar and salt. The same applies to hospital food. A friend who was a patient in a top hospital where heart operations are carried out said that the man in the bed opposite was eating great amounts of cheese as a treat once he could take food after his heart op. I won't even begin to analyse the menus and the excuses, as there is no excuse. Nutrition is based on fact and people who are in positions of power must feed others the *right* foods. They should be required to take a refresher course in the recommended diet for good health.

School dinners cost the taxpayer a fortune – almost £500 million a year – and most offer a minimum nutritional value (school dinner, like the standards of education, varies from area to area). Give children a choice and they will go for the beefburgers and milkshakes everytime – but we must supplement this tasty rubbish with more nutritious foods, especially in an agricultural country such as this where the fruits and vegetables though seasonal, are great.

Perhaps new methods of 'institutional' cooking need to be looked into for those valuable foods not to lose their texture, flavour and vitamins and end up as lukewarm, limp accessories to the greasy beefburger or the overcooked roast.

School milk is a great culprit. The government subsidises full cream milk and a change to semi-skimmed would be beneficial.

Inherited coronary heart disease risk factors, not the genetic and environmental ones are discernible soon after birth and show a particularly dramatic rise between six months and one year. American cardiologists recommend that the fat intake for children should not exceed 30 per cent of the total, of which only one third should be saturated fat. It's not the fish and potatoes and not even the lean meat that are the major culprits – it's the way they are cooked, the fat they are fried in. Changing school menus is a priority. Who will make the start?

GLOSSARY

adrenaline – one of the 'stress hormones' that speeds up the pulse rate; raises blood pressure; increases blood flow to the brain, heart and muscles and raises the metabolic rate. It prepares the mind and body for quick thought and physical action.

aerobics – a type of exercise that elevates the pulse rate for short periods, thereby making the heart beat faster and strengthening it through mild exertion.

angina pectoris – pain in the centre of the chest, which is induced by exercise and relieved by rest and may spread to the jaws and arms. It is caused by poor blood supply to the heart from the coronary arteries. The pain is its call for oxygen and blood. It may be prevented or relieved by such drugs as glyceryl trinitrate and beta-blockers.

atrium – either of the two upper chambers of the heart. The left atrium receives oxygenated blood from the lungs; the right receives venus blood.

atrial tachycardia (see ventricular fibrillation)

autoregulation – the autonomic nervous system – the nervous system is divided into two parts: the voluntary system, and the autonomic – the 'involuntary' system. The latter controls automatic functions such as breathing, heartbeat and the digestive system.

atherosclerosis – coronary artery disease, is a process that begins at birth but does not manifest itself for thirty to seventy years. The artery is hardened and has a fatty material in it called atheromata. It is the most common form of arteriosclerosis which just means 'hardening of the arteries.'

(coronary) angiogram (or cardiac catheterisation) – a tube-like needle is inserted into a vein in the arm or groin and the tip directed into the heart, where a dye is released and the inside of the arteries filmed by complex equipment. It gives a true picture of the progress of coronary artery disease.

arrhythmias – any deviation from the normal rhythm of the heart. Results from the disturbance of the electrical impulses that control heartbeat and will result in palpitations, breathlessness and chest pain. Cardiac arrest or sudden death may occur in more serious cases. Normally caused by heart diseases but also may occur without apparent cause.

atheroma – fatty deposit containing cholesterol which builds up on the inner lining of the arteries over a period of many years. It limits blood circulation and may be symptomless until it blocks blood flow and causes a heart attack. It is caused by a diet rich in animal fats and inherited as well as other environmental risk factors.

beta-blockers – a drug that prevents the stimulation of the beta-andrenic receptors on the nerves of the sympathetic nervous system and decreases the activity of the heart. They are used to control abnormal heart rhythms, to treat angina and to reduce high blood pressure.

blood pressure – pressure of the blood in the main arteries that is needed to push it through the smaller blood vessels. 'Hypertension' is abnormally high blood pressure.

bile salts – bile is secreted by the liver and contains lecithin, cholesterol and bile salts. Bile salts are necessary for the emulsification (making into a liquid) of fats. After they have been absorbed from the intestine they are transported back to the liver for re-use.

caffeine – a drug obtained from coffee and tea, that has a stimulant action, particularly on the central nervous system. It also possesses diuretic properties. It is present in many soft drinks and in large quantities may cause palpitations, nervousness and lack of sleep.

catheter – a tube-like needle inserted into a vein and used to inject and transport substances to specific parts of the body. It is used in a coronary angiogram.

calcium antagonists (or calcium channel blockers) – drugs that interfere with calcium ions, the chemical messengers that make the muscles contract. They allow the coronary arteries to expand thereby carrying more blood to the heart and also depriving the heart of calcium which then enables it to pump less forcefully.

cardiovascular exercise – a type of exercise that helps to strengthen the heart. It must be *Regular* (three or four times a week); *Intense* (raise the pulse rate to an effective, yet safe level for 20 to 30 minutes at a session); and *Progressive* (the stronger you get, the harder the exercise). This type of exercise should always be done with the approval of a doctor.

cerebral haemorrhage – bleeding from a cerebral artery into the tissue of the brain. Caused by a weak blood vessel and high blood pressure.

cholesterol – an organic fat-like substance present in the blood and most tissues. An important part of cell membranes and bile salts. It is synthesised in the liver and concentrated in the blood. An elevated blood concentration is associated with atheroma, of which cholesterol is a major component. It builds up inside arteries causing eventual blockage and heart attack.

chylomicron – a microscopic particle of fat present in the blood.

cirrhosis – a condition of the liver in which the cells deteriorate and die. It is caused by many things including hepatitis and chronic alcoholism.

COMA – abreviation for Committee on Medical Aspects of Food Policy, which produced a report about 'Diet and Cardiovascular Disease' in 1984 recommending a change in the British diet to prevent coronary heart disease.

corneal arcus – a whitish ring around the cornea in the eye, that when present in young people (under 30 normally) may be a symptom of familial hypercholesterolaemia (FH), a genetic condition that causes the body to produce too much cholesterol.

coronary bypass – an operation that replaces one or more of the coronary arteries with a vein from the leg. It is usually performed when the coronary arteries become blocked by a build-up of atheroma, or fat-like substances that prevent the coronary arterial system from providing sufficient blood and oxygen to the heart.

coronary heart disease – a disease where the coronary arteries are gradually and progressively obstructed by the build-up of atheroma, fatty plaque, and if uncontrolled will lead to a heart attack.

coronary spasm – (arteriovascospasm) a spasm in a coronary artery can stop the flow of blood to the heart. The causes of these spasms are not yet known although they are connected with atherosclerosis and blood clots. Chemicals secreted by blood platelets may cause the walls of the arteries to contract thereby inducing spasms.

cholestyramine resin (Questran) – a sequestrant or resin that binds with bile salts, soaking them up so that they are secreted rather than re-circulated into the liver where they will be processed into cholesterol. It is a white powder that is taken orally mixed with water and lowers the blood levels of cholesterol and other fats.

coronary thrombosis – blood clot in a coronary artery blocking the blood supply to part of the heart muscle. and causing a heart attack (also called a coronary).

coronary arteries – small arteries that supply blood to the heart muscle. They branch off from the main artery. the aorta, as it leaves the heart. Atheroma in the coronary arteries is the main cause of heart disease.

coronary angioplasty – a surgical procedure to unblock the arteries. A thin tube (a catheter) is passed from the arm into the blocked artery where a balloon at its tip is inflated to compress the fatty buildup and thereby allow the blood to flow more freely.

diabetes – a disease in which there is an excessive discharge of urine. *Diabetes mellitus* is a chronic diabetes where there is excess sugar in the blood and urine.

defibrillation – a controlled electric shock administered to the chest to restore normal heart rhythm in cases of cardiac arrest due to ventricular fibrillation.

diastolic – the period between two contractions of the heart when the heart muscle relaxes and allows the chambers to fill with blood. It is used for one of the readings taken to measure the blood pressure.

electrocardiogram (ECG) – picture of the electrical impulses made by the beating heart recorded in a simple. painless test.

exercise stress test – a test to measure the electrical impulses made by the beating heart and the changes during exercise. It is usually done on a treadmill or an exercise bicycle with medical supervision a necessity.

fatty acids – make up the blood lipids including triglycerides. Some are made within the body. others must be obtained from the diet.

glucose tolerance – a test used to diagnose diabetes mellitus. The readings indicate the body's ability to use glucose or blood sugar.

gout – a high uric acid level in the blood will cause it to accumulate in joints and cause a painful gouty arthritis. Treatment with drugs has controlled the disease.

heart attack – (myocardial infarction) non-medical term for a sudden serious disorder of the heart in which a part of the heart muscle dies after the blood flow has been interrupted and it has been deprived of oxygen. The patient experiences severe chest pain which may lead to 'ventricular fibrillation' where the heart beats rapidly and out of control.

hypertension – abnormally high blood pressure which increases the risk of heart disease or stroke, if untreated.

hyperlipidaemia – an abnormally high concentration of fats in the blood that can cause 'atheroma', a build-up of fats inside the arterial walls.

familial hypercholesterolaemia (FH) – an inherited condition where the body produces more blood fats, especially cholesterol than is needed. This may cause coronary heart disease if not treated by diet and drugs.

insulin – a protein hormone produced in the pancreas that is important for regulating the amount of sugar (glucose) in the blood. Lack of this hormone causes *diabetes mellitus* which can be treated successfully by insulin injections.

Isometric exercise – based upon the contraction of muscles caused by pulling or pushing against something that does not move and causes resistance and tension in the muscles. (examples of isometric exercises are weightlifting and pushups).

invasive tests – where it is necessary to enter the body to investigate the progress of disease, such as using a catheter in a coronary angiogram.

(HDL) *high density lipoprotein* – all fats combine with protein in the blood to make them soluble, forming lipoproteins. HDL has a low concentration of cholesterol and triglyceride and seems to 'remove' cholesterol from the body.

lipids – natural substances that are not soluble in water. Have high energy value and are associated with vitamins and fatty acids. Blood fats and steroids are lipids.

(LDL) low density lipoprotein – accounts for about 70 per cent of cholesterol in the blood and is responsible for depositing cholesterol on the arterial wall.

linoleic acid – a colourless unsaturated fatty acid large amounts of which are found in corn oil and soya bean oil and in polyunsaturated fats.

ischaemia – poor blood supply usually due to narrowing of an artery.

myocardial infarction – see heart attack

monounsaturated fats – neither raise nor lower cholesterol levels, but are fats and high in calories. They are found in olive oil, peanut oil, avocados and olives.

magnetic resonance scanning – advanced type of body scanner that uses radio pulses and a powerful magnet to produce a picture of the inside of the body with the help of a computer interpretation of the pulses.

menopause – the time in a woman's life where ovaries cease to produce an egg cell every four weeks and menstruation ceases. At this time there is a change in the balance of sex hormones.

laser surgery – recent development in which a laser is beamed through a catheter and used to burn away a substance within the body. It is being developed as an alternative to bypass operations to clear arterial blockage.

noradrenaline – a 'stress' hormone usually released with adrenaline causing the arteries to constrict while increasing the blood pressure and blood flow through the coronary arteries to the heart, preparing the body for quick physical action. Also called 'norepinephrine'.

nuclear scanning – radioactive substances are injected into the body and a computer measures the isotopes and converts the information into a picture of the inside of the body.

neuroendocrine system – controls activities of the body through circulating hormones and the nerves. It is closely linked with the autonomic nervous system which controls the involuntary actions such as the heart beat and intestinal motions.

NACNE – National Advisory Committee on Nutrition Education whose report advised on changes in the national British diet.

oestrogen – female sexual hormones that promote the growth and function of the female sexual organs and characteristics.

obesity – grossly overweight condition, at least 20 per cent heavier than the top of the 'ideal' weight for a person's height.

palpitations – a feeling of 'fluttering' in the chest, usually caused by a faster, stronger or an irregular heartbeat.

PET Scanning (positron emission tomography) – another scanner that uses the radioactive isotopes that are inhaled or injected into the body to create an image by computer interpretation of the change in positron particles in the body metabolism.

pituitary gland – small endocrine gland at the base of the skull that controls hormones for growth and metabolism.

pacemaker – a device that is implanted in the body to regulate the heartbeat and to prevent problems that may result from an extreme and irregular beat.

plasma – the fluid in which the blood cells are suspended.

phospholipid – a lipid that is involved in many of the body's metabolic processes.

plaque – a build-up of fats and fibrous tissue on the inside of arteries that leads to atherosclerosis, or a narrowing of the coronary arteries.

platelets – a structure in the blood responsible for clotting.

platelet clumping – the 'stress hormones' norepinephrine and adrenaline stimulate the blood platelets to clump together and form a clot. They can lodge in the coronary arteries if they form on the inside of an injured arterial wall and thereby obstruct the flow of blood to the heart or in the carotid arteries to the brain (causing a stroke).

endothelial lining – a layer of cells that lines the arteries.

preventive medicine – actions to stop an illness from developing by controlling its causes, as opposed to therapeutic medicine, which is treating an illness or injury after it has occurred.

prostaglandins – a family of chemicals that control the process of clotting. Thromboxane A_2 is one of these.

polyunsaturated fats – thought to be less harmful to the heart and arteries than saturated fats and may even be beneficial as they are thought to reduce saturated fats in the blood. They are present in fish oils and certain vegetable oils such as sunflower, safflower, soya and corn oil.

radioisotope – a substance which emits radiation during its decay into another element and which can be 'traced' within the body to create a picture of the area to be diagnosed.

stroke (cerebral thrombosis) – a paralysis or malfunction due to the lack of blood flow to the brain, caused by a clot (thrombosis) in or a rupture (haemorrhage) of a cerebral artery.

saturated fats – dietary fats thought to be harmful to the heart and arteries if eaten in too great a quantity over a period of time in a person whose blood cholesterol level is higher than normal. They are found in dairy products like butter, cream, cheese and creamy milk; in meat and meat products, in lard and some vegetable oils like palm oil and coconut oil. Also usually found in oils that are merely labelled as 'vegetable oil', where the type of oil is not identified.

stress – general term for psychological pressures which may affect the chemicals in the body and may result in coronary heart disease.

serum cholesterol – a medical term for the amount of cholesterol in the blood.

thromboxane A_2 – a potent chemical which promotes clotting and which is sometimes produced by the stress hormones. It can result in the creation of blood clots that cause a blockage in either the coronary or cerebral arteries.

streptokinase – an enzyme that is capable of dissolving blood clots. It is injected into the body to treat the blockage in an artery after a heart attack or stroke.

TPA (tissue-type plasminogen activator) – a new drug manufactured by genetic engineering which activates 'plasminogen' that does the actual clot-dissolving. It can be valuable in treating heart attacks and strokes if it is developed as anticipated.

systolic – period of the cardiac cycle where the heart contracts and expels the blood from the heart. Used for one of the readings taken to measure the blood pressure.

Type A personality – a classification of people who may be 'coronary-prone' because of their highly aggressive personality. They are competitive, hostile, with many other observable stress inducing characteristics.

Type B personality – another behavioural classification to identify those less at risk for CHD. They are more relaxed, unhurried. less ambitious and less 'time conscious'.

triglycerides – made from the digestion of dietary fats and are a form in which fats are stored in the body. A high level of triglycerides may indicate a potential for CHD.

VLDL (very low density lipoprotein) – secreted by the liver and carrying cholesterol and triglycerides made in the liver. Its production is stimulated by excessive alcohol consumption and in overweight individuals. It contributes to the formation of plaque on the arterial wall.

uric acid – a component of the urine that is deposited as

crystals in the joints of people suffering from gout.

xanthoma – a yellowish swelling, nodule or plaque in the skin resulting from deposits of fat and usually accompanied by a raised blood cholesterol level. They are usually found on the buttocks, knees, or on joints and in tendons.

xanthelasmas – a yellowish deposit of fatty material in the skin around the eyes.

ventricle – either of the two lower chambers of the heart. The left ventricle receives blood from the pulmonary vein and pumps it into the aorta. The right ventricle pumps blood into the pulmonary artery.

ventricular fibrillation – a rapid and chaotic beating of the heart that becomes too fast for the heart to pump blood properly. The heart beats out of control, is not supplied with oxygen and stops beating.

FOOD CHART

I have found most of the food charts given in nutrition and diet books bewildering. In many cases it is not the fault of the authors because it is almost impossible to create a uniform system to evaluate the fat contents of different foods in the various amounts we eat them. Articles adorned with fancy wheels and charts, complex tables and graphs, usually make us turn the page quickly. Therefore, to supplement the information already given, the following list separates foods into very general areas of: 'Advisable'; 'In Moderation'; and 'Un-Advisable'.

The chart is concerned only with the saturated fat levels in each of the foods. For the purpose of this book we are not evaluating the salt, sugar, fibre, calorie or mineral contents of the foods. It is a 'general' chart; for more specific numbers and percentages you should consult a book that sets out the precise scientific and chemical breakdown of foods (I recommend *The Composition of*

Foods, by McCance and Widdowson, published by HMSO, which is the book that most nutritionists refer to) or speak with a dietician.

All foods should be eaten 'in moderation' for a well-balanced diet (unless you are suffering from a specific illness tha requires you to alter your diet more drastically) so my classifications are general, based upon my personal experience, and your own discretion should be used to decide how much is moderate. And remember that *moderate* means just that – it is not a licence to eat as much as you like of these items. The chart should be used as a guide and with this knowledge and your own 'conscience' you should be able to lower your fat intake to an acceptable level. An added bonus to cutting down your intake will of course be a loss of weight.

DAIRY PRODUCTS

In my *moderation diet* I have substituted skimmed milk for full fat milk. Cream is avoided except as a very occasional treat in cake or trifle. Eggs are to be eaten in moderation.

Advisable	*In Moderation*	*Not Advised*
Skimmed milk	Semi-skimmed milk	Full fat milk
Egg whites	Eggs (try to limit	Cream
Cheese	to 3–4 a week)	Coffee whiteners
Cottage & low fat	Edam, Parmesan	Excess egg yolks
curd cheese	(it is high in fat	Cheddar, Cheshire
Reduced fat	but we normally	Stilton,
cheeses, such as	sprinkle it rather	Full-fat Cream
St. Ivel Shape,	than eating a large	Cheese
Tendale, Sains-	piece)	
bury's (own brand),	Medium-fat	
Quark	Camembert and Brie	
	Cheese spreads,	
	Processed cheese	

Most of us enjoy cheese but the hard, high-fat cheeses

such as cheddar and very creamy cheeses should be a 'treat' only, and should not be eaten as a regular, every day habit. Cut down on the amount of cheese you eat.

FATS & OILS

Earlier in the book I mentioned that *all* oils are high in calories and fat, and this includes butter, corn oil and the margarines that are high in polyunsaturates – but it is the *type* of fat that matters to us. Saturated fat is the fat to be avoided, though your consumption of fats of any kind should be reduced. Some oils have less saturated fats than others, therefore if you must fry foods, at least fry them in sunflower, safflower or soya oil. Many supermarkets have their 'own brands' of these types of oils. Avoid lard, any animal fat and any 'vegetable oil' that doesn't tell you exactly what it contains (read the label carefully) as some vegetable oils, such as palm oil and coconut oil, are very high in saturated fats. Only use an 'advised' oil in making salad dressing and avoid bottled dressings that don't state the type of oil and fat they contain.

Advisable	*In Moderation*	*Not Advised*
All fats should be limited	Flora margarine, or any other margarine labelled 'high in Polyunsaturates' Low-fat spreads such as St. Ivel Gold, Outline, supermarket's own brands, corn oil, sunflower, safflower oil, soya oil, olive oil	Butter dripping, suet, lard, 'hard' margarine or any not 'high in polyunsaturates', vegetable oil, unlabelled as to type of oil it contains palm or coconut oil

CAKES, PASTRIES & BISCUITS

All cakes, pastries, biscuits and puddings made with whole milk, eggs or unsuitable fat or oil are not advised, but as they are a part of our lives and pleasure, should be eaten in *moderation*. Avoid 'cream-filled' cakes and remember that although jam and sugars in general contain calories and will put on weight, they don't contain saturated fats – so if you must eat a doughnut – eat one that is jam-filled, rather than cream-filled. Home made or shop-bought cakes and biscuits made with wholemeal flour and suitable margarines or oil are lower in saturated fats than most others.

DESSERTS

Skimmed milk puddings, low fat puddings such as jelly (made with water) sorbets, skimmed milk sauces or those made with yoghurts are advisable. Custard made with whole full cream milk and eggs is high in saturated fat.

Advisable	*In Moderation*	*Not Advised*
Skimmed milk puddings, low fat puddings, jelly (made with water) sorbets, skimmed milk sauces, low-fat yoghurts	Desserts made with suitable margarine or oil non-dairy ice-cream	Tinned or whole milk puddings, dairy ice-cream cheesecake custart tarts fresh cream desserts trifle, cream puddings chocolate bars

BREADS & CEREALS

Wholemeal bread and wholegrain foods are best. Fancy breads, such as croissants are made with lots of butter and are 'treats' not everyday delights. Pasta and rice are high in fibre and carbohydrates and low in fat – especially good if the rice is brown and the pasta made with wholemeal. But in all cases, including cooked beans, it is the *sauce* that contains the saturated fats. Remember that a vegetable sauce made with little added fats or meat is better.

Advisable	*In Moderation*	*Not Advised*
Wholemeal flour, oatmeal, wholemeal bread, wholegrain rice and pasta, breakfast cereals high in bran and low in fat such as Weetabix, Shredded wheat, All-bran, porridge oats	White flour, white bread, low fibre 'white' cereals, cornflakes, sugar coated breakfast cereals, white rice, white pasta, crumpets	Fancy breads, such as croissants, savoury cheese biscuits cream crackers fried bread

SWEETS, PRESERVES & SPREADS

Advisable	*In Moderation*	*Not Advised*
Marmite Bovril	jam, marmalade, honey, sugar, fruit pastilles, peppermints, etc.	Peanut butter, chocolate spread, lemon curd, mincemeat, chocolate, toffees, fudge, coconut bars

165

SALADS & SAUCES

Advisable	*In Moderation*	*Not Advised*
Fresh vegetable salads, with little dressing made from 'advisable oils', vinegar or lemon Low-fat yoghurt dressing Soy sauce	Tomato ketchup, brown sauce, sweet pickle, coleslaw (not creamy), low-fat or slimmer's salad dressings (check oil content)	Salad cream, mayonnaise, salads made with mayonnaise or salad cream bottled salad dressing unless stated 'high in polyunsaturates'

MEAT & POULTRY

Meats contain saturated animal fats. The cuts you choose must be lean and before eating cut off *all* visible fat. Try not to add oil while cooking, and grill rather than fry. Bacon with less white fat (back or gammon) is better than streaky. Poultry is preferable to meat, but remember the skin contains a lot of saturated fat and the dark meat is fattier than white.

Advisable	*In Moderation*	*Not Advised*
Chicken turkey, rabbit, game	Lean: Ham, beef, pork, lamb, bacon lean mince Veal, liver & kidneys occasionally Boiled ham	Visible fat on meat (including crackling) poultry skin streaky bacon, duck, goose, sausages, beefburgers Luncheon meat, pates & liver

sausage. salami.
corned beef.
cornish pasties
and meat pies.
pork pies. sausage
rolls. black
pudding

FAST FOODS

Most fast foods are 'griddled' (fried on a flat griddle in
their own fat. rather than 'grilled' where the fat burns off or
drips through the grill away from the meat). Even if they
are 'all beef' the total fat content may be very high. Fried
chicken is heavily saturated in cooking oils as are fried fish
and chips. Normally we don't know what type of oil our
chips are fried in. and unless the oil is low in saturated fats.
the fried food will be coated in saturated fats and be very
bad for you. Potatoes are good – it's the fat they're fried in
that makes them bad.

FISH

Advisable	*In Moderation*	*Not Advised*
All white fish. oily fish. e.g. herrings. tuna. mackerel. tuna canned in brine grilled fish fingers	Shellfish occasionally (boiled or grilled. no butter or cream sauce) oysters. raw mussels winkles tuna and sardines canned in oil (but drain away the oil)	Fried scampi. fried fish fingers. fish roe. any fish fried in oil that is 'not advisable' fish cakes fish pastes

167

NUTS

Advisable	*In Moderation*	*Not Advised*
Walnuts	Almonds. brazil nuts. chestnuts. hazelnuts. peanuts	Coconut

FRUIT & VEGETABLES

Advisable	*In Moderation*	*Not Advised*
All fresh & frozen vegetables including peas. broadbeans. sweetcorn	Chips. if cooked in suitable oil or fat (large size rather than crinkly or very thin) avocados, olives	Potato crisps chips cooked in unsuitable fat or oil
Dried beans and lentils are particu-high in fibre.		
baked potato – with skin		
baked beans (the tomato sauce is high in sugar but the fat content is low		
boiled potatoes (it's the butter you add that contains the fat)		
fresh fruit		
dried fruit (high in calories)		

DRINKS

Advisable	*In Moderation*	*Not Advised*
mineral water	tinned or packet	cream soup

168

fruit juices, clear	soups
soups, homemade	Alcohol
soups such as	Malted drinks
vegetable & lentil	such as Horlicks,
	Ovaltine

PERCENTAGE OF TOTAL FAT

Meat & Meat Products

Salami	46%	
Fried streaky bacon	45%	
Grilled streaky bacon	36%	
Sausage roll (flaky)	36%	
Grilled lamb chop	29%	
Pork pie	27%	
Luncheon meat	27%	
Liver sausage	27%	
Roast lamb (shoulder)	26%	
Fried pork sausages	25%	
Cornish pastie	21%	
Steak & kidney pie (individual)	22%	
Roast leg of pork	20%	
Black pudding, fried	22%	
Fried beefburgers	17%	
Roast leg of lamb	18%	
Minced beef	13%	
Grilled rump steak	12%	
Casseroled pigs liver	8%	(but high in cholesterol)
Stewed steak	7%	
Fried lambs kidneys	6%	(but high in cholesterol)

Poultry

Chicken, meat & skin	14%
Chicken, roast, light meat	4%
Chicken, roast, dark	7%
Turkey, roast, light	2%
Turkey, roast, dark	4%

Duck, roast, meat & skin	29%
Rabbit, stewed	8%

Fish

Tuna, canned in oil	22%
Fried scampi	18%
Smoked mackerel	16%
Sardines, canned in oil	14%
Fried fish fingers	13%
Grilled kippers	12%
Cod fried in batter	10%
Fish paste	11%
Steamed plaice	2%
Steamed haddock	1%

Cheese

Cream cheese	50%
Stilton	40%
Cheddar	34%
Parmesan	30%
Processed cheese	25%
Camembert	23%
Edam	23%
Cheese spread	23%
St. Ivel Shape (cheddar-type)	17%
Cottage cheese	4%
Tendale cheddar	15%
cheshire	14%
Medium-fat curd cheese	11–15%
Low-fat skimmed milk cheese or Quark	0.5%
Full-fat curd cheese	23–28%

Milk, Butter, Oils

Oil (all kinds)	100%
Lard	99%
Butter	82%
Margarine (all kinds)	80%

Double cream	50%
Single cream	21%
Dairy ice cream	7%
Gold-top milk	5%
Silver-top milk	4%
Yoghurt	1%
Skimmed milk	Less than 1%
Low fat spreads	40%

HEART ATTACK!
WHAT TO DO?

1
A heart attack happens when the blood supply to the heart muscle is cut off. This causes considerable pain in the chest which might spread to the neck, jaw or arm. Someone with a heart attack may also feel faint, giddy or sick. YOU CAN HELP HIM RECOVER OR EVEN SAVE HIS LIFE.

2
Often, all you need do is help sit him down like this. Try to prop his back and knees and loosen his belt and tie. Keep him warm but do not use a hot water bottle. Do not give anything to eat or drink. Call a doctor or dial 999 and ask for an ambulance.

3
If he becomes unconscious, you must find out if he is breathing.

4
Put your ear to his mouth. Can you hear or feel the breaths? Can you see his chest or stomach moving? If you are not sure, look at the inside of his bottom lip. If it is blue, he is not breathing.

5
If he is breathing and still unconscious, put him in the recovery position, like this. If you can, get help then return and watch him in case he stops breathing.

6
If he is not breathing, make sure there is nothing blocking his mouth or throat. Use your finger to clear out any obstruction or vomit.

7
Lie him on his back. Bend his head backwards with one hand and push his jaw up with the other hand. This may start him breathing. If not, pinch his nostrils together, seal your lips around his open mouth and blow in. Watch his chest rise as you blow in.

8 Take your mouth away and watch his chest fall. Blow in three more times.

9 Now check if his heart is beating. Put two fingers in the groove at the side of his Adam's apple and press firmly. Can you feel a pulse there? If the heart's beating, continue mouth-to-mouth breathing. Give one breath every three or four seconds. Continue this until he starts breathing on his own.

10 If you can not feel a pulse or if his face has turned very white or purple, then his heart has stopped. Lie him on his back on the floor or on firm ground and kneel down alongside.

11 Find the bottom of his breastbone and place your hands like this on the spot. Press down hard about 1½ inches (4 cm), then release. Press down again and repeat this 60 times a minute. To help you keep time, count out: "one thousand and ONE, one thousand and TWO, one thousand and THREE, one thousand and FOUR". Press down hard on every number. After 15 presses, stop and give two mouth-to-mouth breaths. Keep up this routine – 15 presses and two breaths – but stop after about three minutes to see if the heart has started beating. Check his pulse to find out.

12 **HAND POSITION**

13 If there is someone else's there, ask them to help you. They can do the presses, while you give mouth to mouth. They can give five presses, then you give one breath. After one minute, check his pulse to see if the heart has started. **14** If the heart starts, stop pressing. Keep on with mouth-to-mouth breathing until he starts breathing. When he starts breathing on his own, turn him onto his side into the recovery position. **15** While you are waiting for the doctor or ambulance, watch him all the time in case his heart stops again.

GET HELP QUICKLY

999

PROMPT ACTION MAY SAVE A LIFE

ARTHRITIS
Relief Beyond Drugs
by RACHEL CARR

If you are one of the many thousands of people who suffer from arthritis you will know that drug therapy is essential for certain conditions – but by itself that is not always enough. Impaired mobility and the emotional effects of chronic pain can be greatly reduced, and sufferers helped to come to terms with their condition by following a daily routine of the stretching and limbering, deep breathing and relaxation exercises described in this book.

Rachel Carr, at one time severely disabled by osteo-arthritis, now tells you what simple techniques she used herself. The exercises are straightforward and varied so that every arthritis sufferer can benefir from them.

0 552 99033 7   £1.95